THE MIND OF VOLTAIRE

A Study in his "Constructive Deism"

THE MIND OF VOLTAIRE

A Study in his "Constructive Deism"

by

Rosemary Z. Lauer, Ph.D.

THE NEWMAN PRESS

Westminster, Maryland

1961

Nihil obstat: EDWARD A. CERNY, S.S., S.T.D.
          Censor Librorum
Imprimatur: FRANCIS P. KEOUGH, D.D.
          Archbishop of Baltimore
May 1, 1961

The *nihil obstat* and *imprimatur* are official declarations that a book or pamphlet is free of doctrinal and moral error. No implication is contained therein that those who have granted the *nihil obstat* and *imprimatur* agree with the opinions expressed.

To
S.J.T.

Foreword

IN THE PHILOSOPHICAL SYSTEMS of those thinkers who have asserted the existence of God, there is scarcely any more crucial problem than the question of the relationship existing between God and the universe. What a philosopher maintains about this relationship either determines or is determined by what he maintains on all sorts of other questions, notably the questions of the nature of the material universe and its laws, the existence and nature of human freedom, and the nature of God. Consequently, in assaying a systematic presentation of Voltaire's philosophy, it has seemed wise to give special attention to this focal problem of the relationship existing between God and the universe, especially in view of the fact that the term *deism*, which is quite justly applied to Voltaire's thought, connotes, above all else, a position on this matter.

Deism, however, is a term broad enough and varied enough in its meanings to cover a number of quite divergent intellectual enterprises. There are, nonetheless, certain minimal conditions required that the term may be applied justly to anyone's religious or philosophical thinking: the author must eschew Christian revelation or regard it as only a reformulation of a natural religion known through reason alone; he must offer arguments proving, from observation of the world of nature, that God exists; he must show by reason that God rules the world of nature by eternal, immutable laws; and, finally, he must explain how practicable rules of morality can be deduced from knowledge of nature and man's place in nature.

If a deistic body of thought is concerned principally with destroying the traditional Christian conception of revelation as a genuine and special manifestation of God to man, it may be called "critical deism." If, on the other hand, the principal concern is with the construction of a rational explanation of man's relation to the universe and to God, the deism may be called "constructive." [1] Or, it is possible to refer to one and the same deism as "critical" in those parts which aim at destroying revealed religion, and as "constructive" in those parts which are directed toward a natural explanation of the ordered universe, a natural morality, and a natural religion. It is in this latter sense that Voltaire's deism is referred to as "constructive"; the use of the term is not to be interpreted as a denial that Voltaire engaged in the "critical" phase of deism, but only as an indication of the limits to be observed in this study. That is, we shall be concerned, not with Voltaire's attacks on traditional Christianity, but only with his theories regarding the world of nature, of which man and his values constitute the most interesting part, and the relation of this world of nature to God.

---

[1] "Critical deism" and "constructive deism" are terms used by Leslie Stephen in his *English Thought in the Eighteenth Century* (2 vols., New York: G. P. Putnam, 1927) as titles of chapters iii and iv, volume I. Stephen, unfortunately, gives no definition there of "critical deism" or "constructive deism"; however, an analysis of the chapters in question appears to justify using the terms in the way in which they are used in this study.

Preface

VOLTAIRE IS ONE OF THOSE famous men whose mind we think we know so well that we fail to acquaint ourselves with any details of it. He is the first victim of his own colorful life and gift for the stinging repartee, since they encourage us to go no deeper than the surface impression. We are familiar with Frederick the Great's portrait of Voltaire as a man who was "constitutionally hot and atrabilarious, meagre-visaged, with an ardent and penetrating look, and a quick and malignant eye." And the image comes readily to mind of him as an old man coming back to Paris for a final triumph, and replying from his coach to the question of whether he carries any contraband: "Only myself." We may well have laughed at the ridiculous Dr. Pangloss for seeing teleology in the close relation of legs with trousers or noses with spectacles, and may have felt the lash behind the science-fiction adventures of Micromegas (Mr. Small-Big from the star Sirius), as he observes the warring human insects on our ball of mud. And in any case, we can still hear that strident note—half war cry, half mania—which rings throughout Voltaire's last decade of writing: "Crush the infamous thing." His campaign against organized religions seems to embody the spirit of the Enlightenment in its assault upon the Church and the religious orders.

Yet these impressions do not enable us to take the full measure of Voltaire's thought. They do not yield the indispensable information about his intellectual formation and development or about the personal unity of conviction to which he came. We are left with many unanswered questions, such as why Voltaire remained on relatively peaceful and even friendly terms with the Jesuit teachers and editors until he was about sixty years old, and then why he outdid the Encyclopedists in the ferocity and persistence of his attacks. Only the careful and converging work of scholars in many fields is beginning to weave together the various strands of evidence into the pattern of this complex mind and social power. We are probably not quite ready yet for a definitive synthesis of all these aspects. For in some areas, especially philosophy, there is a good deal of further exploration to do toward understanding Voltaire in his age.

He did fill the scene in Enlightenment France as one of its most versatile and durable men of letters. The range of his literary forms was remarkably broad. Voltaire did noteworthy work in plays which were produced, an epic poem and much light verse, historical studies, an unfortunate excursion into Biblical commentary, and a one-man philosophical dictionary. Especially in the didactic letter and the philosophical tale, he found appropriate modes of expression for his philosophical ideas, which were imaginatively conceived and usually developed in an informal way. Voltaire is not an historian precisely in our sense of the word, but his studies in that field moved in the direction of a deliberate use of primary sources, reminiscences, interviews, and materials taken from the social and cultural spheres, rather than narrowly from the military and political side. With the recent developments in the history of science, we are beginning to appreciate also his contribution toward the spread of Newton's natural philosophy in France. Voltaire devoted about five years of his early life to an intensive study of contemporary English science, especially the many adaptations of Newton's thought. This enabled him to write a fairly well-informed popularization of the Newtonian scientific conception of the world.

The investigations in these several fields have pointed up the need for a fresh appraisal of Voltaire's philosophical positions. We might suppose that there would be an abundance of competent books dealing with this side of his thought, but such is not the case. Some of the general studies in French and English do include a descriptive account of his philosophical ideas, but this is usually done from the literary standpoint and in the context of other matters. Anyone familiar with the Voltaire scholarship sees the need for a detailed and separate treatment. The threefold requirement is for a book which concentrates upon his philosophy for its own sake, analyzes it in a genuinely philosophical way, and also makes intelligent use of the historical findings of other scholars. On all three counts, Dr. Rosemary Lauer's work meets this need in Enlightenment studies and the history of modern philosophy. It ferrets out the main line of Voltaire's philosophical thought, without neglecting its connections with his other interests. In doing this, Dr. Lauer holds strictly to her task of elucidating and evaluating the doctrine on philosophical grounds, without becoming distracted by other issues which in the past have prevented a patient analysis of the philosophical argument itself. And finally, her book makes a good start in relating the philosophical aspects to findings made in other approaches to Voltaire.

In his book on the elements of Newton's thought and in his much revised manuscript treatise on metaphysics, Voltaire elaborated some basic principles which guided all of his later speculations. He was deeply influenced by Locke and profited by a critical reading of Descartes and Malebranche, Pascal and Bayle, Leibniz and Wolff. On the matter of method, Voltaire gave his preference not to the synthetic-deductive method but to the analytic-inductive way. From an analysis of the scientific and the common sense descriptions of man and the world, he worked out some fundamental positions and claimed for them a high degree of probability. His minimal theism kept him apart from the materialist wing of the Enlightenment, but difficulties about evil led him to speculate that God is limited in power and acts always out of necessity. Radicalizing Locke much more than the English philosopher intended, Voltaire also treated man as a thinking sort of matter, whose actions are necessitated but voluntary (or performed by his own will), and whose life is probably snuffed out at death. Both on this score and that of repudiating Christian revelation as divine truth, he kept his distance from Christianity. In Voltaire's own words, the essential message of all religions is the same and amounts to this: "There is a God, and one must be just." From this narrowly rationalistic viewpoint, everything else about our human religious life seemed to be either superfluous or repressive.

Dr. Lauer provides a well-ordered introduction to the main themes in Voltaire's thought. She is careful to follow his order of an inductive development based on scientific and ordinary notions about the physical world and man the knower and moral agent. Yet this entire discussion is oriented toward Voltaire's theory about God. This is truly the heart of his philosophical efforts, the central concern around which his other views are organized. Dr. Lauer's honest and pointed exposition and critique

of the Voltairean teaching on God and the universe will percepti-
bly deepen our understanding of this major Enlightenment
figure. It will also encourage our making a calm appraisal of those
many aspects of American life which still bear the imprint of
Voltaire and his colleagues.

Saint Louis University   James Collins

Table of Contents

Table of Abbreviations

D. P., *Dictionnaire philosophique*

Eléments, Eléments de la philosophie de Newton

Q. E., *Questions sur l'Encyclopédie*

Traité, Traité de métaphysique

THE MIND OF VOLTAIRE

A Study in his "Constructive Deism"

CHAPTER ONE

The Mind of Voltaire: Its Formation

IT IS a truism that "no one philosophizes in a vacuum"; that is, that there are exerted upon every formulator of a philosophical system various influences which, even though the philosopher be unaware of them, predetermine to some degree the method and content of his philosophic work. In Voltaire's case, these influences can be reduced to two general ones: the *Zeitgeist* of the age in which Voltaire lived, and the intellectual formation which was proper to Voltaire himself. It is proposed, therefore, to consider briefly these two general determinants of Voltaire's constructive deism.

The Age of the Enlightenment, which gave birth to Voltaire, was itself the fruit of several centuries of ideological gestation, whose stages of development involved a gradual detachment of the European mind from a dependence on divine revelation as a source of truth, and a growing conviction that the book of nature could be read with greater understanding than the book of the Scriptures. From having been satisfied that God's being in his heaven was a sufficient guarantee that all was right with the world, some men had come to hold that no one could possibly be certain that God *was* in his heaven unless it could be seen in the universe that all *was* right with the world.

The principal causes at work in this change of mental outlook were three: a negative cause and two positive ones. Negatively, the sixteenth-century challenge to the papacy as the divinely-appointed custodian and interpreter of revelation was the beginning of a widespread loss of confidence in Scripture as a guide for the discovery of truth or the conduct of life. If a passage in the Bible may legitimately be interpreted in as many ways as there are readers, then only a limited number of pathways are open to those who consider the matter seriously: one may replace the rejected papal infallibility by another authority, by a presbytery, a synod,

or even a civil ruler; one may cease to regard Scripture as valuable
in the intellectual order and assign to it instead a vague emotional
or inspirational function, but with its source in a personal God
revealing himself to man; or one may simply relegate the Bible to
that group of classical works whose authorship is shrouded in the
mists of antiquity. In the latter case, the books would have historical interest, certainly, and would still function as a font of sage
observations about human life. Their degree of veracity, however,
would be determined by the approved methods of historical research, and the degree of confidence which might be placed in
their comments on human life and its conduct would be limited
by their verification in the collective experience of mankind. It
was this latter way which was chosen by the *philosophes* of eighteenth-century France. Having rejected divine revelation as a
source of understanding of their universe, they were in need of a
substitute.

Concurrently with the gradual loss of confidence in Scripture
on the part of large segments of sixteenth- and seventeenth-cen-
tury Europe, a substitute was being supplied by the scientific discoveries of such men as Copernicus, Kepler, Galileo, Francis
Bacon, and Newton. Though the type of experimental work done
by these men had never been totally lacking during the medieval
period, the development of new instruments of research, the tele-
scope and the microscope, opened up to scientists two entirely
new ways of observing the macrocosmos and the microcosmos.
Fascinating though Galileo's observations about the pendulum and
falling bodies might have been, they were seen in an entirely new
light and raised to an entirely new order when Newton's theory
of gravitational attraction revealed the possibility that the entire
universe might be explained in terms of such simple mathematical
propositions as Galileo had recognized in the behavior of weights
sliding down an inclined plane. If one could construct a mechanical model reproducing to scale the movements of the celestial
bodies, if one need only posit a mutual attraction of these bodies
to one another to explain the movements of each of them, then
one might very well hope that answers to all questions about the
material universe could be given with as much clarity and simplicity. Scripture no longer needed to assure man that his universe
was an orderly, a rational, one. Rather, in cases in which there appeared to be a conflict between scriptural statements and the find-

ings of the new science, the elated confidence which the men of the Enlightenment possessed in the latter led them to regard the apparent conflicts as further evidence of the merely human authorship of the Scriptures and the consequent deficiencies of the sacred writings.

In addition to the discoveries of the new sciences, perhaps the most potent force directing Europe toward the spirit of the Enlightenment was the epistemological writing of John Locke in his *Essay Concerning Human Understanding*, which became the "psychological gospel of the eighteenth century." [1] The epistemology of innate ideas and principles was uprooted in such wise that it has never since then exerted its former influence. Though Locke was not at all the first European to write that man enjoys no natal or prenatal gift of divinely infused ideas and judgments, he was the first to say so in such an easily understood fashion and to such a large and enthusiastic audience. As Carl Becker so succinctly puts it: "This was Locke's great title to glory, that he made it possible for the eighteenth century to believe with a clear conscience what it wanted to believe, namely, that since man and the mind of man were shaped by that nature which God had created, it was possible for men, 'barely by the use of their natural faculties,' to bring their ideas and their conduct, and hence the institutions by which they lived, into harmony with the universal natural order." [2] Reason, not in the Cartesian sense of an ability to judge about a complexus of God-given ideas, but in the Lockean sense of a power to judge correctly about sense experience, was truly enthroned. Robert R. Palmer, in his *Catholics and Unbelievers in Eighteenth-century France*, calls Lockean empiricism "Proposition One" of the Enlightenment: "Sensationalism was not only a psychology but a metaphysics, and not only a theory of knowledge but a theory of human nature." [3]

This new fascination with the information the senses convey

---

[1] Carl Becker, *The Heavenly City of the Eighteenth-century Philosophers* (New Haven: Yale University Press, 1932), p. 64.

[2] *Ibid.*, p. 65.

[3] Robert R. Palmer, *Catholics and Unbelievers in Eighteenth-century France* (Princeton: Princeton University Press, 1939), p. 131. See also Charles Frankel, *The Faith of Reason, the Idea of Progress in the French Enlightenment* (New York: King's Crown Press, 1948), p. 42. Voltaire himself writes in a letter to Jean Baptiste Nicolas Formont, c. August 15, 1733, that he has left the chords of his lyre—poetry and drama—for philosophy, but that

about the world resulted in a change of attitude with respect to the relative merits of the sciences and their methods. In an intellectual atmosphere in which clear and distinct ideas are the ultimate aim and in which the ideas are thought to be implanted in man's soul independently of his contact with a world of extended objects, that branch of science which would be regarded as the most worthy of attention and the model in methodology for all others could be nothing but mathematics. And such was the case in France in the early eighteenth century, when Cartesianism had come to be looked upon as orthodox. Once the empiricism of Locke was accepted, however, there had to be, and was, a general enthusiasm for physics, chemistry, and biology. This enthusiasm did not relegate mathematics to the limbo of the otiose, but only to the sphere of instruments useful in the investigation of nature, especially in the newly developed physics. Inasmuch as this latter science concerned itself with what Locke had termed the primary qualities, the objectively real, physics enjoyed a pre–eminence over the other natural sciences. The latter were oriented toward the secondary, or subjective, qualities and hence could not hope to render such a mathematically perspicacious account of their objects as could physics.[4] It was the physicist Newton, then, with his refusal to lay down nonempirical hypotheses, his insist-

---

he doubts anyone but Locke has much of value to say: "I have left it [literature] for what is called philosophy, and I am quite fearful that I have left a real pleasure for the shadow of reason. I have reread the reasoners: Clarke, Malebranche, and Locke. The more I read, the more I am confirmed in the opinion I've had that Clarke is the best sophist that ever was, Malebranche the most subtle romancer, and Locke the wisest man. What he has not clearly seen I despair of ever seeing. He is the only one, in my opinion, who does not presuppose at all what is in question" *Correspondence*, edited by Theodore Besterman (Les Délices, private publication, 1953), III, 127. This edition of Voltaire's correspondence covers, in the volumes printed to date, only the years 1704 to 1764. When completed, the edition will contain seventy volumes, in which 20,000 letters will be printed. Of these, five thousand are being published for the first time. In this study, letters written before 1765 are cited from the Besterman edition; for the succeeding years, the Moland edition has been used.

[4] Paul Hazard, *European Thought in the Eighteenth Century*, translated by J. Lewis May (New Haven: Yale University Press, 1954), pp. 130–31: "Geometry lost the supremacy it had at one time enjoyed, because people came to the very definite conclusion that it added nothing to the stock of knowledge. All it did was to develop, to add, by deduction on deduction, to principles already securely established. Thus it had no contact with reality. . . . Descartes had had his day. At the moment it was Newton's turn. Newton had enlisted mathematics in the service of Natural Science."

ence on observation, on measurement and the mathematical analysis of measurement, who became the leading scientific spirit of the Enlightenment, and the second great positive influence in shaping the *Zeitgeist* of that period. "Because he [Newton] had started, not from abstractions, not from axioms, but from actual fact to arrive at further facts, duly authenticated; because, for the laws of Nature he had gone to Nature herself, the rising generation had made him one of their heroes." [5]

All these innovations of the Enlightenment had what might be termed their consummation, however, in the new religion, a religion for which no divine inspiration was claimed or desired other than that which men drew from the newly understood universe in which the wise might read the divine plan. There was no longer any reason why one should look to a Book, or to a Church, for an assurance of God's existence, for an explanation of his nature, or for a set of directions for human conduct. Just as there is no watch without a watchmaker, so the deists said, there could be no Newtonian universe without a divine mechanic; the size and mathematical precision of the great machine were sufficient to indicate the power and intelligence of God. The very nature of man, if seriously considered, would reveal a natural, and therefore right, pattern of conduct.[6] Revealed religion, with its scientifically inaccurate documents, with its failure to produce the millennium, or even a reasonable degree of peace among the sects into which it had been divided, could very well be dispensed with. The "enlightened" man, so hopeful now of having the entire universe explained to him in propositions as simple and all-embracing as Newton's theory of gravitational attraction, could no longer be expected to accept on faith religious doctrines which could not be understood equally simply and exhaustively.

In accordance with this new outlook in religion, there appeared in the eighteenth century a large number of books written for the express purpose of proving from nature that there is a God. To be sure, not all of them were written by men who rejected the tradition of divine revelation, but they were, nonetheless, a symptom of the times, an indication of the new *Zeitgeist*. Many of those who retained their own confidence in Scripture

---

[5] *Ibid.*, p. 131.
[6] *Ibid.*, p. 114.

were concerned that the growing number of those who did not share this confidence should be convinced of the existence of God. The following titles are indicative of the type of natural investigation which was pursued for the purpose of convincing the wavering or the "enlightened":

- W. Derham, *Physico-Theology, or a demonstration of the being and attributes of God from his works of creation,* London, 1713.
- W. Derham, *Astro-Theology, or a demonstration of the being and attributes of God from a survey of the Heavens,* London, 1715.
- B. Nieuwentijdt, *Het Regt Gebruik der Werelt Beschouwingen,* Amsterdam, 1715.
- B. H. Brockes, *Irdisches Vergnügen in Gott,* Hamburg, 1721–43.
- J. J. Scheuchzer, *Physica sacra,* Augsburg, 1731–35.
- J.-A. Fabricius, *Hydrotheologie,* Hamburg, 1734.
- Fr.-Chr. Lesser, *Lithotheologia,* Hamburg, 1735.
- Fr.-Chr. Lesser, *Testaceo-theologie,* Leipsig, 1744.
- Abbé Noël-Antoine Pluche, *Le Spectacle de la nature,* Paris, 1732–50.
- J. H. Schutte, *Anthropotheologie, wie man Gott aus der Betrachtung des Menschen erkennen könne,* Halle, 1769.
- Th. Morgan, *Physico-theology, or a philosophico-moral disquisition concerning human nature, free agency, moral and divine Providence,* London, 1741.[7]

There seems to be reflected in this collection of titles the peculiar combination of optimism and desperation experienced by many who attempted to embrace the new learning while clinging to the certainties of the old religion.

Despite the avalanche of arguments proving the existence of God, not everyone among the wavering was converted. Such men as Baron Holbach and LaMettrie came to regard Voltaire as a "bigot" because the latter insisted that at least some of the theists' arguments were conclusive. How Voltaire, equally with

---

[7] These titles have been selected from a list given by Paul Hazard, *La Pensée Européenne au XVIIIᵉ siècle, de Montesquieu à Lessing* (3 vols., Paris: Boivin, 1946), III, 51. A list of strictly scientific works published in the eighteenth century is given in Margaret Sherwood Libby's *The Attitude of Voltaire to Magic and the Sciences* (New York: Columbia University Press, 1935), pp. 274–83. These two lists of titles might be regarded as an abridged history of European thought in that century.

Holbach and LaMettrie a product of the eighteenth-century
Zeitgeist, could differ so profoundly from them in his philosophical conclusions can be explained, not by the general religious and scientific trends of the times, but only by those influences peculiar to Voltaire, especially by his education.

Voltaire received a formal education which was limited to a
few years spent at Louis-le-Grand, where, until he was sixteen,
he received the classical training for which the Jesuit school-
masters were noted. If any philosophic studies were pursued,
there is little evidence of the fact in the *philosophe's* writings.
Rather, it seems that any philosophical encounter between
Voltaire and the Jesuits at Louis-le-Grand was limited to correspondence during the 1730's, concerning the possibility of
"thinking matter." The letters Voltaire received in answer to his
queries indicate that any training in philosophy which might
have been given at the Jesuit school would have been Cartesian in
content.[8] It was not, however, only at school that Voltaire was
educated. As Norman Torrey remarks, "His real education . . .
in the broader French sense of the term, was in the salons of his
mother's society and under the tutelage of her more intimate
friends, the Abbés Gédoyn and Châteauneuf." [9] This tutelage, it
would seem, had its consequences largely in inspiring Voltaire
with the spirit of the Enlightenment, but also in directing his
attention to authors who expounded that spirit. It is in knowing,
then, who these authors were that one can learn the direction
Voltaire's studies took and how they helped determine his philosophic convictions.

It is quite evident that, while Voltaire was familiar with the

---

[8] For Voltaire's letters to Fathers Porée and Tournemine, see the Besterman edition of the *Correspondence:* c. November, 1730, II, 142; c. June 13,
1735, IV, 77–79; December 13, 1735, IV, 207; December, 1735, IV, 211–220;
November 17, 1738, VII, 453; c. December 31, 1738, VIII, 138–39.

[9] Norman Torrey, *The Spirit of Voltaire* (New York: Columbia University Press, 1938), p. 16. Torrey adds a note on these two abbés and the society
in which they lived: "Unlike the Jesuit teachers, the abbés had accepted not
only the literary forms and stylistic excellencies of their favorite Latin authors, but also the very spirit of pre-Christian culture. The Renaissance was
slowly extending its influence to fields other than the literary field. The easy-
going Epicureanism and Stoicism of Montaigne had never died but had been
revived in the salon of Ninon de Lenclos and had made tremendous inroads
on the externally Christian France of Louis XIV. Voltaire's *libertinage* was
thus in no sense a revolt against the teachings of his Jesuit masters. Under
them he merely went to school; his education was a somewhat different matter." *Ibid.,* p. 17.

names of some of the ancient masters of philosophy, he had only
the most casual acquaintance with their writings. True to the
spirit of the age, he had so little confidence in the past's ability to
teach the man of the Enlightenment that it seems never to have
occurred to him to read seriously his ancient and medieval predecessors in philosophy. As Voltaire himself writes, anyone who
has once read Locke, or who is his own Locke, must find Plato a
babbler. In philosophy, "a chapter of Locke or of Clarke is by
comparison with the prattling of antiquity what the *Optics* of
Newton is compared with that of Descartes." [10]

Nor did Aristotle fare much better. In fact, though Voltaire
preferred Aristotle as the lesser of two evils, Aristotle suffered at
Voltaire's hands in a way almost entirely spared to Plato: Voltaire
undertook a popular exposition of Aristotle in the *Philosophical
Dictionary*. As a consequence, anyone who chanced to be intro-
duced to Aristotle by Voltaire could only wonder why Aristotle
bothered to write down the things which Voltaire attributes to
him. We are told that Aristotle taught that the principles of bodies
are three: matter, form, and privation. Matter is the "first principle" of everything, the subject of everything, indifferent to
everything. Form is essential to matter's becoming any definite
thing. Privation, according to Voltaire's interpretation, is that in
a being which distinguishes it from all those things which it is
not, so that one can say the form's making the matter into a definite thing deprives the matter of whatever would make it any

---

[10] Voltaire in a letter to Pierre Joseph Thoulier d'Olivet, February 12,
1736, *Correspondence*, Besterman, V, 57. The editions of Voltaire's works
most often cited throughout this study are the following: *Oeuvres complètes*, edited by Louis Moland (52 vols., Paris: Garnier, 1877–85), and the
Dictionnaire philosophique, edited by Julien Benda from the text established by Raymond Naves (Paris: Garnier, 1954). References to the Moland
edition will include the name of the work, the date of publication if the
date has been established, and the volume and page numbers; e.g., *Lettres
de Memmius à Cicéron* (1771), Moland, XVIII, 456. Citations of the *Dictionnaire philosophique*, when the Naves text is used, will note the name of
the article, the date of publication the first time the article is cited, and the
page numbers; e.g., "Morale" (1767), *Dictionnaire philosophique*, Naves,
pp. 325–26.

A special bibliographical problem arises in connection with the *Dictionnaire philosophique*, for the title has been used by various editors to cover a
multitude of articles; how large the multitude is depends often on little more
than the editor's whim. Voltaire himself used the title for a collection of articles arranged alphabetically and published in 1764 (but dated 1765) in Geneva. The composition of the articles was begun in 1751 or 1752, and, as the

other thing.[11] This, of course, is not absolutely contrary to what
Aristotle teaches, but there is no evidence that Voltaire really understood the Aristotelian doctrine. Rather, there seems to be evidence that Voltaire imagined matter, "prime matter," to have an
independent existence apart from form; that he imagined the
form to be some pre-existent entity put into the pre-existent

third word in the original title, *Dictionnaire philosophique portatif*, indicates, Voltaire's purpose was to provide a more succinct substitute for
Bayle's lengthy and weighty *Dictionnaire historique et critique*. Between
1764 and 1776 there were ten editions of this *Dictionnaire philosophique portatif*, several of the editions, including the one published in 1769 as *La Raison
par Alphabet*, being enlarged, corrected, or annotated editions of the original of 1764. A number of the articles published in the early editions of the
Dictionnaire were subsequently published again as part of the series, *Questions sur l'Encyclopédie*, between 1770 and 1774. To complicate matters still
further, the editors of the Kehl edition of Voltaire's *Oeuvres complètes*
(1785–1789) included under the title of *Dictionnaire philosophique* the original *Dictionnaire*, the *Questions sur l'Encyclopédie*, the articles contributed
by Voltaire to the *Encyclopédie* and to the *Dictionnaire de l'Académie*,
the *Opinion par Alphabet*, and about sixty other shorter works which had
never formed any part of an alphabetically arranged publication. The arrangement of the *Dictionnaire philosophique* in the Moland edition, which
is the one used throughout this study for articles not included in the Naves
text, follows that of the Beuchot edition of 1828–1840. That is, it includes as
part of the *Dictionnaire* just about everything included by the editors of
the Kehl collection except the sixty or so articles which had never formed
part of an alphabetical work. These latter, Beuchot and Moland have
relegated to a section called *Mélanges*. The Naves text includes under the
title, *Dictionnaire philosophique*, only the articles which Voltaire himself
published under the title *Dictionnaire philosophique portatif*. In the copious
notes, however, articles from the *Questions sur l'Encyclopédie* are included
when they treat of the same topics as the *Dictionnaire* articles. References
to these notes will appear, for example, as "Ame" (1770), *Questions sur
l'Encyclopédie*, Naves, p. 424. When the Moland *Dictionnaire philosophique*
is cited, the citation will include the name of the article, the name of the
work in which the article was first included by Voltaire, the date of first
publication, and the volume and page numbers; e.g., "Platon," *Nouveaux
Mélanges* (1765), Moland, XX, 230. If the article was never part of a larger
collection, the citation will read, for example, "Athée," *Dictionnaire
philosophique*, Moland, XVII, 455. In the latter case, the title, *Dictionnaire
philosophique*, is not intended to designate anything other than the section
in the Moland edition where the article is to be found. In the Moland edition, volumes XVII to XX inclusive cover the *Dictionnaire*.

Raymond Naves' work, *Voltaire et l'Encyclopédie* (Paris: Presses
Modernes, 1938), pp. 169–84, gives a helpful list of the articles Voltaire wrote
for the *Encyclopédie* and a list of the variants in the articles published in the
Encyclopédie and the same articles published by Voltaire himself in the
Dictionnaire philosophique, the *Questions sur l'Encyclopédie*, and the *Nou-
veaux Mélanges* of 1765.

Throughout the remainder of this study, the *Dictionnaire philosophique*
shall be referred to as *D.P.* and the *Questions sur l'Encyclopédie* as *Q.E.*

[11] "Aristote" (1770), D.P., Moland, XVII, 370.

matter; and that he supposed "privation" to be a third entity, whose function it was to keep out all the qualities which would tend to make matter anything other than what the form was actually making it to be. Aristotle's physics, Voltaire announces nevertheless, "must certainly have been very deficient in its details.[12] The ancients, he says, did not possess the necessary instruments of investigation, and so they reasoned about what was below the cliff on which they stood, though they could never *see* what was contained in the abyss. However, Voltaire finds that Aristotle can be misquoted to the benefit of the critical deist: the ancient philosopher had said that "Incredulity is the beginning of wisdom." [13] This is somewhat different, it would seem, from saying that "philosophy begins in wonder," but it was much more conducive to the triumph of reason over revelation.

Nor did the centuries closer to Voltaire's own enjoy a more flattering evaluation. Of St. Albert the Great, he wrote, "Albert was surnamed 'The Great' because he lived in an age in which men were very small." [14] Albert's pupil, St. Thomas Aquinas, fared scarcely better. In a passage which can hardly be explained as anything other than a deliberate fabrication or a colossal misunderstanding, Voltaire states that St. Thomas taught there were three souls in man: the "psyche" in the breast, the "pneuma" distributed throughout the body, and the "nous" in the head. This, Voltaire says, was the only doctrine on the soul in the schools until his own time, and it would have gone hard with anyone who mistook one of St. Thomas' souls for another.[15]

---

[12] *Ibid.*

[13] *Le philosophe ignorant* (1766), Moland, XXVI, 51. In *Voltaire and the English Deists* (New Haven: Yale University Press, 1930), p. 203, Norman Torrey notes numerous instances in which Voltaire misquoted from the English deists or ascribed to them passages they never composed: "Toland and Collins were accorded an almost even break between true and false attributions." "In *La Bible enfin expliquée* (1776), he [Voltaire] quotes 'les incrédules,' and with rare lapses into truthful citation, gives as authorities any name or list of names that comes into his head." *Ibid.*, p. 13.

[14] *Eléments de la philosophie de Newton*, Moland, XXII, 490.

[15] "Homme" (1771), *Q.E.*, Moland, XIX, 384–85. Also "De l'Ame" (1765), *Mélanges*, Moland, XXIX, 338–41, and "Ame" (1770), *Q.E.*, Moland, XVII, 139. In *Le Philosophe ignorant* (1766), Moland, XXVI, 64–65, we are told that St. Thomas says of God that He is "nature and supposit, that He exists essentially, participatively, and noncupatively"! In the *Summa Theologica* I, q. 76, a. 4, St. Thomas gives his reason why there could be no more than one form, or soul, in man. *Opera omnia* (Rome, 1882—), V, 223–24.

While Descartes could not (like Plato, Aristotle, and St. Thomas) be disdained as having lived in an age of ancient or medieval foolishness, he and his followers were considered by Voltaire to be of no greater use than their predecessors. Descartes, Spinoza, and Leibniz had rejected Locke's "Proposition One"; rather, they were unaware of such a proposition, and so they continued the practice of making philosophical pronouncements without having any experimental knowledge to provide a foundation. A particularly enlightening passage in a letter to Nicolas Claude Thieriot reveals, not only Voltaire's attitude toward Spinoza, but also the *philosophe's* general attitude toward serious study of philosophical writings:

It was indeed a very hard task for me to find that damn'd book which, under the title of *Improvement of humane reason,* is an example of nonsense from one end to the other, and which besides, is a tedious nonsense and consequently very distateful to the French nation, who dislikes madness itself when madness is languishing and flat. The book is scarse, because it is bad, it being the fate of all wretch'd books never to be printed again. So j spent almost a fortnight in the search of it, till at last j had the misfortune to find it. 20m. J hope you will not read thoroughly that spiritual nauseous romance; tho indeed you deserve to read it to do penance for the trouble you gave me to enquire after it, for the tiresom perusal j made of some part of this whimsical stupid performance, and for your credulity in believing those who gave you so great an idea of so mean a thing.[16]

---

[16] Letter of March 11, 1727, *Correspondence,* Besterman, II, 48. (The English and the spelling are Voltaire's own.) In connection with this topic, Helen Temple Patterson writes in the introduction to her edition of the *Traité de Métaphysique* (Manchester: Manchester University Press, 1937), xiii, "It is worth noting that Spinoza is only represented in Voltaire's library at Leningrad by the *Réfutation* of Boulainvilliers (1731)." See also the section on Spinoza in Voltaire's article, "Dieu," *Q.E.,* Naves, pp. 511–13. Paul Hazard, in an article entitled "Voltaire and Spinoza," *Modern Philology,* XXXVIII (February, 1941), 351–64, attempts to show that Voltaire acquired a new interest in Spinoza about 1765, but that Voltaire could never regard Spinoza's system as other than dangerous, for it lent itself more readily to the materialism of a Holbach than to the deism of a Voltaire. In his *Lettre à M.L.C.* of 1768, Moland, XLVI, 205, Voltaire uses a phrase which sounds quite Spinozistic: *tu es le seul Etre, tout le reste est mode.* But as late as 1771 Voltaire wrote that he had "always believed that Spinoza did not often understand himself and that that is the principal reason why he is not understood." "Dieu-Dieux" (1771), *Q.E.,* Moland, XVIII, 367.

The degree to which Voltaire was influenced by Leibniz is summarized succinctly by W. H. Barber in two sentences:

> The formative period for his attitude to Leibnizian metaphysics is from 1736 to 1744; after that Voltaire's mind is made up, his opposition to Leibniz, Wolff, and their followers has crystallized into a set of views to which he gives expression whenever occasion demands, but which no new interest in the subject ever impels him to revise. . . . His knowledge of Leibniz is neither systematic nor profound, and it apparently served only to confirm him in his earlier beliefs concerning the futility of metaphysical speculation, and to strengthen his allegiance to the ways of thought of Newton and Locke.[17]

It was in virtue of Voltaire's failure to understand Leibniz' theory that this is the best possible world that he was able to write the scathing anti-Leibnizian satire found in *Candide*. It was Voltaire's ardent conversion to Locke which made it inevitable that the French *philosophe* should treat only with ridicule the doctrine of pre-established harmony.[18]

George Berkeley was one further object of Voltaire's ridicule. According to Voltaire's perhaps deficient understanding of Berkeley's *Three Dialogues*, Hylas might have escaped the trap set for him by Philonous, had Hylas simply admitted that man knows nothing of the subject of extension, solidity, divisibility, mobility, figure, etc., and had he asserted that the subject is not any the less real for man's ignorance of it.[19] In short, Berkeley is one who, "by a hundred captious sophisms pretended to demonstrate that bodies do not exist," or that "ten thousand men killed by ten thousand cannon shots are only ten thousand apprehensions of man's understanding." Berkeley's errors, following from his

---

[17] W. H. Barber, *Leibniz in France, from Arnauld to Voltaire* (Oxford: Clarendon Press, 1955), p. 197, p. 89. Barber notes that Voltaire's knowledge of Leibniz was obtained from two sources: the Leibniz-Clarke correspondence and a translation of the *Monadology*. *Ibid.*, p. 186. Mme. du Châtelet had a considerably better appreciation of Leibniz, which she incorporated into her *Institutions physiques*. It was largely in reply to her *Institutions* that Voltaire composed his *La Métaphysique de Newton, ou Parallèle des sentiments de Newton et Leibnitz*, published in 1740 and later printed as the first part of the *Eléments de la philosophie de Newton*.

[18] See *Eléments de la philosophie de Newton, passim*; Barber, *op. cit.*, pp. 172–86; and Voltaire, *Exposition du livre des Institutions Physiques* (1740), Moland, XXIII, 129–46.

[19] "Corps," *D.P.*, Moland, XVIII, 270. (Beuchot estimates that this article was written between 1765 and 1770. See Moland, XVII, viii–ix.)

failure to distinguish properly between primary and secondary qualities, are not, Voltaire says, even worth refuting.[20]

To complete the picute of Voltaire's intellectual background, it is necessary to mention a number of French works which were circulated in manuscript form in France for twenty or thirty years before they were published, about 1750. An anonymous essay entitled *Pensées sur la religion dont on cherche de bonne foy l'éclaircissement*, also known as *Doutes sur la religion* and *Examen de la religion*, was included by Voltaire in his *Recueil nécessaire* of 1765. The *Pensées sur la religion* contains almost nothing of "constructive deism"; its content is almost entirely along the lines of "critical deism." The guiding principle in the work is the premise that every man must be permitted to examine and judge his religion; indeed, he *must* do so. Following a discussion of the nature of true religion, there are six chapters presenting the customary deistic criticisms of Scripture, of original sin, of the Trinity, and of the historicity of the prophecies and the life of Christ. The conclusion of these criticisms is that God has not revealed to man a particular religion or cult; certainly not the Christian religion, for the internecine wars of Christians have tended to destroy society, and Christianity has failed to serve as a moral check on its adherents. The work ends with a paean to the supreme being who has given reason to man, and with the assertion that the two guides for human life are reason and the maxim, "Do unto others as you would have them do unto you." [21] Another clandestinely circulated work, almost identical in content with the *Pensées*, the *Analyse de la religion chrétienne*, written possibly by Dumarsais, was also known to Voltaire. Its conclusion, like that of the *Pensées*, consists of a passage glorifying reason and another advocating the practice of the "golden rule." [22]

A document even more important than the preceding ones is the *Testament de Jean Meslier*, which became known to Voltaire

---

[20] *Ibid.*, pp. 270–72.

[21] Clifford M. Crist, *The Dictionnaire philosophique portatif and the Early French Deists* (Brooklyn: S. J. Clark, 1934), p. 25. See Ira O. Wade's article on the *Epître à Uranie*, *Publications of the Modern Language Association*, XLVII (December, 1932), 1082–83, for the similarity of ideas in the *Examen* and the *Epître*.

[22] Crist, *op. cit.*, pp. 26–27. See also I. O. Wade, *The Clandestine Organization and Diffusion of Ideas in France from 1700 to 1750* (Princeton: Princeton University Press, 1938), p. 163.

in 1735 and was published by him in abbreviated form in 1762.[23] Meslier had died about thirty years before the latter date, leaving behind him a "will" in which he declared that he had been ordained a priest only to please his parents, and that throughout his years of acting as pastor of a village church he had not been able to believe the dogmas he preached from the pulpit. Though it is difficult to admire a man who came no closer to possessing the courage of his convictions than did Meslier, it may be said to his credit that his written record is an excellent expression of the materialistic, deterministic atheism which became the fashion in some French circles with the publication of Holbach's *Système de la nature*. There is, in the *Testament*, an introduction damning the political and religious authorities who made it so unpleasant and even dangerous for an unorthodox thinker to express his views. Meslier then proceeds to enunciate the principal doctrines of deism: religion is entirely of human origin; Christianity, for the same reasons as given in the *Examen de la religion* and in the *Analyse de la religion chrétienne*, cannot be accepted by thoughtful men; the doctrines of the Trinity, the Incarnation, and Transubstantiation are philosophically untenable; the Christian search after pain and suffering, and the Christian injunction to love one's enemies are so much nonsense; men are by nature equal, and the differentiation of social status is the result of abuses in society; matter is uncreated; beings are possible or impossible in themselves and not by reason of a divine will; evil is as necessary as everything else in the universe; the spirituality and immortality of the soul cannot be proved.

In addition to the foregoing propositions, which could be held by a deistic thinker and were accepted by Voltaire, Meslier proposes a number of statements which stamp him as a radical materialist and atheist. Not only is matter not created, but there has been no creation at all; beings, which are all material, have motion of themselves and not from any external "first mover"; if there were a God, then the imperfections, vices, and deformities in nature could not be explained; nature and the laws inherent in matter explain the universe insofar as it can be explained. Even here, Voltaire follows Meslier to some extent. For Voltaire,

---

[23] Crist, *op. cit.*, pp. 27–31. See also Voltaire, *Extrait de Sentiments de Jean Meslier* (1762), Moland, XXIV, 293–336. For a detailed study of the influence of Meslier on Voltaire, see Andrew R. Morehouse, *Voltaire and Jean Meslier* (New Haven: Yale University Press, 1936).

too, admits no creation in the Christian sense of the term, and he asserts the eternity of the universe. However, Voltaire denies that matter has motion of itself, but insists that it receives motion from God; moreover, the very laws of nature are imposed on it by a geometrizing God; and, finally, the imperfections in nature prove only that God was not able to produce "the best of all possible worlds." [24] Newton's influence was stronger than Meslier's.

One further French influence, whose importance in Voltaire's intellectual development can scarcely be over-rated, was Pierre Bayle, whose own philosophical views were shaped in large part by Montaigne. Bayle supplied Voltaire not only with a philosophical point of view, but also, in his *Dictionnaire historique et critique*,[25] with a literary form demonstrated to be popular and effective for the presentation of philosophical ideas. Helen Temple Patterson states in the introduction to her edition of the *Traité de Métaphysique* that Voltaire owned a copy of the 1697 edition of Bayle's *Dictionary*, which he kept always at his desk.[26]

Besides being influenced by the writings of Locke and Newton, who were the principal sources of the Enlightenment *Zeitgeist*, Voltaire's thought was determined in a minor way by the writings of several other Englishmen: Shaftesbury, Mandeville, Toland, Collins, and Bolingbroke. The contribution of Shaftesbury can be seen in Voltaire's ethical theory; the effect of Mandeville's *Essay on the Origin of Moral Virtue* and *Fable of the Bees* is evident in the same area, but principally in that part of ethics which deals with the genesis of society. Toland's chief contribution would appear to be a general attitude toward "natural religion" as opposed to a religion dependent upon revelation. Anthony Collins exerted his greatest influence through the *Philosophical Enquiry Concerning Human Liberty*, which was apparently the deciding factor in Voltaire's final renunciation of any true freedom in human conduct. Margaret Sherwood Libby cites some of the doctrines Voltaire may have gathered from Bolingbroke: the value of observation and experiment, the exist-

---

[24] Ira O. Wade, *The Clandestine Organization and Diffusion of Ideas in France from 1700 to 1750*, p. 93.

[25] The first edition of Bayle's *Dictionnaire historique et critique* appeared in 1697, published in Rotterdam. The second edition, the last to appear before Bayle's death in 1706, was printed in the same city in 1702. In form, the *Dictionnaire historique et critique* was modeled on the *Grand Dictionnaire historique* of Moréri, first published in Paris in 1674.

[26] Helen Temple Patterson, *op. cit.*, xii.

ence of design in the universe as a proof of the existence of God, the reality of final causes, the potentialities of reason as a means of improving mankind, and the judgment that Aristotle, Descartes, and Malebranche wrote only nonsense.[27]

It appears, then, that Voltaire, being a man peculiarly impressed with the spirit of his times, permitted himself to be influenced, not by those who spoke from the past, but only by those of his own age, those who spoke as his contemporaries, those who themselves were animated with the Enlightenment *Zeitgeist*. These influences having been considered, it remains to see what their consequences were in the *philosophe's* constructive deism. In accordance with the empirical spirit Voltaire so highly recommends, we shall begin our study of God's relation to the universe, the question about which constructive deism revolves, by considering that term of the relation which is immediately evident through the senses: the world of nature.[28]

---

[27] Margaret Sherwood Libby, *op. cit.*, p. 21. See also Norman Torrey, *Voltaire and the English Deists*, for a thorough evaluation of the contributions of Toland, Collins, Woolston, Tindal, Chubb, Bolingbroke, Middleton, and Annet.

[28] Because of the great difficulty of knowing when, in his literary works, Voltaire is presenting his own position and when he is merely presenting an idea for consideration, only very slight use is made of the dramas, tales, and poems. That is, in this study, the conclusions proposed shall be based almost solely on the more ostensibly philosophical works of Voltaire.

CHAPTER TWO

The Material Universe

THE MATERIAL UNIVERSE INCLUDES, for Voltaire, all those things which are extended: inanimate objects, plants, animals, and men. Inasmuch as all these things are alike in being material, they can be considered in their materiality and in abstraction from those characteristics by reason of which they differ from one another. For Voltaire, such a consideration involves a number of questions strongly reminiscent of the Aristotelian four-cause approach to scientific investigation.

In a dialogue between a philosopher and "Nature," which is taken as designating all that there is except the Great Being,[1] Voltaire portrays the philosopher as putting to nature a number of questions about herself. These questions suggest a plan of procedure in investigating Voltaire's notion of nature, because they are the very problems the author attempts to solve in his writings on this subject. First of all, what *is* nature? Is it composed of parts? If so, of what are the parts composed? Is nature eternal? Does it have any force of itself? Can the force which nature has be diminished? Is matter necessary; if not, why does it exist? [2]

Our problem, therefore, can be dealt with by pursuing an elaboration of these same questions. Accordingly, consideration will be given in turn to each of the following topics: the nature of matter, whether it is essentially composite, whether it is essentially extended, whether it is infinite, whether it is eternal; the nature of motion; whether it is of the essence of matter to be in

---

[1] "Nature, Dialogue entre le philosophe et la Nature" (1771), *Q.E.,* in *Dialogues et anecdotes philosophiques,* edited by Raymond Naves (Paris: Garnier, 1940), pp. 369–71.

[2] Despite Voltaire's contempt for the schoolmen, his questions amount to the stock Aristotelian queries concerning formal (what is it?), material (of what are its parts composed?), efficient (is nature eternal?), and final (why does it exist?) causes, plus one concerning the properties (does it have any force of itself?).

motion; the nature of space and time, whether they are "absolutes"; final causality in the material universe; and the question of whether there is any hierarchy, or "chain," of material things.

The influence of Locke's theory of knowledge makes it impossible for Voltaire to attempt an answer to the question of the very essence of material nature,[3] but in the *Elements of Newton's Philosophy* there is a rather superficial examination of some answers of earlier philosophers, followed by an attempt to justify a theory closely resembling that of Empedocles, but with a larger number of elements.[4] There is no purpose, says Voltaire, in attempting to decide who was most ridiculous: Thales, who made water the principle of everything; Heraclitus, who reduced everything to fire; or the atomists, who attempted to explain everything as composed of cubes piled one upon another and turning about among themselves. The most remarkable explana-

---

[3] "Ignorance" (1765), *D.P.*, Moland, XIX, 424: "J'ignore ce que c'est la matière." See also "Matière" (1764), *D.P.*, Moland, XX, 51: "We weigh matter, we measure it, we decompose it, and if we seek to advance one step beyond these gross operations, we find ourselves powerless, and before us an immeasurable abyss."

[4] *Eléments de la philosophie de Newton*, Moland, XXII, 427-33. The *Eléments de la philosophie de Newton* was first published in 1738, the original edition containing only the Newtonian physics. Three years later, Voltaire published *La Métaphysique de Newton*. In 1741 the two publications of 1738 and 1741 were combined in one volume, *Eléments de la philosophie de Newton*, the *Métaphysique de Newton* forming the first part and the original *Eléments de la philosophie de Newton* forming the second and third parts. There were subsequent editions of the complete text in 1748 and 1756. The 1756 edition added a chapter on the "freedom of indifference." The edition used by Moland is the one of 1748, but with the 1756 additional chapter on freedom. The second and third parts, the parts dealing almost exclusively with physics, do not concern us here, and so the variations in these parts can be ignored. The variations in the first part, the part dealing with "metaphysics," are almost exclusively merely literary; the one important change relevant to this study is the addition of the chapter on the freedom of indifference. Throughout the remainder of this study, the *Eléments de la philosophie de Newton* shall be referred to as *Eléments*.

See Robert L. Walters, *Voltaire and the Newtonian Universe, a Study of the Eléments de la philosophie de Newton* (Thesis: Princeton University, 1955), for the scientific background of Voltaire and the history of the composition of the *Eléments*. Unfortunately for the purposes of this study, Walters concentrates on the scientific content of the *Eléments* and limits to about five pages (217-21) his consideration of the philosophical First Part. In her Columbia University Thesis, *Newton's Law of Attraction and the French Enlightenment*, 1950, pp. 51-62, Ruth Murdoch gives an analysis of Voltaire's thought on Newton, as expounded in the *Eléments*.

tion in the past was the Aristotelian one, which posited prime matter, the same throughout, indifferent to and capable of all forms. Just as metal, on being molded, may become an urn or a statue, so this prime matter, being formed somehow, becomes the various things of this universe. Not only was this the opinion of Descartes, Voltaire continues, but even of the great Newton, who, however, can be excused for falling into error in this matter, for Newton's conclusion was the result of an experiment which seemed to show that water had been changed into earth.[5] Descartes, on the other hand, could not have failed to err, for his reasoning was purely *a priori*.

Even though it was the best of the ancient and medieval lot, Voltaire found it necessary to reject the theory of prime matter for several reasons. Prime matter was something of which he could not form any idea, and, therefore, something whose existence he ought not admit. While it was true that he could think of an extended substance without determining his thought to any one kind of substance, any extended substance which really existed would have to be of some determinate kind. Similarly, he could conceive of a triangle without thinking it to be equilateral or scalene or isosceles, but any existing triangle would have to be one of these types. These facts alone, Voltaire says, are sufficient to destroy the theory of prime matter.[6]

Further, if matter, somehow put into motion, sufficed for producing all the things we see on earth, there would be no reason why a little dust stirred up in a container should not produce men and trees, or anything else found in nature; nor why wheat that is sown should not grow into whales. Since these things do not occur, it follows that there are as many different elements, each having been designed, as there are species of

---

[5] Robert Boyle's assistant had boiled some water and found a residue which he took to be earth. He and others concluded that the water had been changed into earth. Boerhaave corrected that error.

[6] Voltaire's understanding of prime matter was notably deficient inasmuch as Aristotle and St. Thomas, probably the two greatest exponents of the prime matter theory, never claimed that one could picture prime matter or even think of it apart from substantial form; much less would they have conceded the possibility of its existing by itself. For the Aristotelian theory of prime matter and substantial form, see Aristotle, Physics, Book A, cc. 6–9, *The Works of Aristotle,* translated by W. D. Ross (11 vols., Oxford: Clarendon Press, 1928–31), II, 188–92.

things. Without this design, matter and motion could produce only chaos.[7]

Observation, too, shows us that, right from the start, the various species of things differ from one another. Minerals, vegetables, and animals are all formed entirely differently; each kind of being is a world of its own. Far from a blind matter producing everything by motion, it is very close to the truth to say that God has formed an infinite variety of beings by infinitely varied means.

In addition, a more careful observation of the world reveals that some mixtures, such as vegetables and animals, can be decomposed and certain minerals obtained from them. Other things, however, can never yield anything unlike themselves: from gold only gold can be obtained; from mercury, only mercury; sand, mud, and pure water have never been able to be changed into any other species of being. The only possible conclusion, then, is that vegetables and animals are composed of elementary particles, which are not themselves decomposable. The elementary particles are the various minerals, earth, sand, fire, air, water, sulphur, and the like; composite beings are made up of these unchangeable elements.[8]

---

[7] It seems difficult to believe that Voltaire could have so completely misinterpreted Aristotle's hylomorphic theory as to confuse the "first act," or form, of a thing with movement, but it is even more difficult to interpret this passage otherwise. In the article, "Aristote" (1770), *D.P.*, Moland, XVII, 367–72, Voltaire goes into some detail in an interpretation of the hylomorphic theory. Though to the eighteenth-century Frenchman the statement that the principles of bodies are matter, form, and privation may seem to be egregious nonsense, that is simply due to a language difficulty. Eighteenth-century Frenchmen use these terms differently from the way in which they were used in Aristotle's Athens. Matter is the first principle of every body, its subject; since matter is indifferent to becoming one thing rather than another, form is required to determine it to become some certain thing. Privation is the absence of that which would make a thing other than it is; for example, when matter has become a rose, it is deprived of whatever would make it silver or lead. This observation, however, Voltaire says, is so trite that it is scarcely worth repeating. Then, without explaining the meaning of "form," the author proceeds to an explanation of Aristotle's definition of motion, "l'acte de ce qui est en puissance." By this phrase, Voltaire says, Aristotle means only to say that matter can be moved, and, very likely, that motion is not essential to matter. The whole of the *Dictionnaire* article seems to be either an amazingly naive interpretation of the Aristotelian theory or an indirect attack on Holbach by stressing the fact that there is design in nature and that motion is not of the essence of matter.

[8] In *Des Singularités de la nature* (1768), Moland, XXVII, 172, Voltaire writes that the change of one being into another being, a substantial change,

There seems to be only one possibility that elementary particles, such as salt, should become elementary particles of gold: the annihilation of the salt and the creation of the gold. One can see that this is necessarily true if one thinks of the immutability of the various species, for such immutability requires that the species be composed of immutable principles. The immutability of the species, however, usually seems to be taken for granted by Voltaire. Nevertheless, in the *A.B.C.* of 1762, he did offer an argument against any possible evolution of the specific kinds of minerals, plants, and animals: if thumbs exist today, they must have existed always, for, if there is a reason for their existence today, there must always have been a reason. "If they are useful, they ought always to have been; from the fact that a species exists, it follows that that species has always existed . . . God is acting, and so he has always acted. . . . Men, snakes, spiders, oysters, and snails have always existed because it was always possible that they should exist." [9]

The immutable, constituent principles of the immutable species can be immutable only if they are perfectly solid, and, consequently, always the same shape. As such, they cannot become any other element, for, by reason of their hardness, they cannot receive any different configuration. However, where there is question of explaining the nature of the elements themselves, it is extreme audacity, the *philosophe* writes, for man to attempt an explanation. Newton, though he attempted such an explanation, at least had the grace to make it a humble one. The elements of matter, which serve as the bases of all the things produced in our universe, are material; that is, they are extended and impenetrable beings which God can, but does not, divide *ad infinitum* or annihilate. Leibniz, on the other hand, was sufficiently temerarious to pretend that he understood the very nature of these elements and

---

would be only the annihilation of the first thing and the creation of the second. Therefore, it is absurd to imagine that one element could become another.

[9] *L'A.B.C.* (1762), Moland, XXVII, 396–97. There seems to be a Leibnizian flavor to the latter part of this argument, insofar as it seems to attribute to a possible being some conatus toward existence. However, what Voltaire seems to mean is actually something more Spinozistic: the various species are possible because the divine nature is such that it necessarily causes them; because God is eternally active, he eternally effects whatever it is that his nature determines him to effect. Because the divine nature does not change, there is no change in the possibility or actuality of the existence of the various species.

undertook to explain their extension. What was worse, he attempted to explain *extension* as a consequence of *unextended* monads. He supposed extension to result from simple beings, whose nature it was to have unconscious perceptions of the past, present, and future. Not only is this explanation ridiculous in its consequence that the most loathsome things would then be chock-full of ideas of the entire universe, but, Voltaire says, it is also a violation of the principle of noncontradiction. That is, there is no comparison between simple beings, such as the monads are supposed to be, and extended beings; but one would certainly expect that a thing should be in some respects like that of which it is composed. Leibniz' notion is as monstrous as that of those who maintain that gold is composed of several elements of iron, or sugar of colocynth.[10]

As for Wolff's theory that composite beings are made up of simple beings which have neither figure nor size and cannot fill space, Voltaire thinks the position could be overthrown by the following propositions. A composite being is necessarily divisible *ad infinitum*, and that is proved geometrically. If it is not physically divisible *ad infinitum*, that is only by reason of a lack of sufficiently fine instruments. Of course, if one divides or decomposes the primary germ of men and plants, there will be neither men nor plants; that is, if there are to be men and plants, there must be undivided bodies. Nevertheless, these primary germs are divisible in fact; they are not simple, without extension. If they were simple and without extension, they would not be bodies, and it would be surpassingly strange if bodies were formed from things which were not themselves bodies.[11]

While he must disagree with Wolff, Voltaire esteems him; but with Berkeley's views, it is another matter. Had Berkeley confessed his ignorance, he would have saved himself from proving it to the world. In telling the world that bodies have neither colors nor odors, nor warmth, but that these modalities are merely in our sensations, he was merely repeating something

[10] *Eléments*, Moland, XXII, 432–34. Voltaire appears to employ here the principle of noncontradiction in a rather unique manner, though Anaxagoras before him had argued similarly when he asked how it could be possible that water should come from nonwater, etc.

[11] Letter to Crown Prince Frederick of Prussia, c. April 25, 1737, *Correspondence*, Besterman, VI, 125–26.

which was already quite well-known. But from there, he went on to extension and solidity (which Voltaire regards as the *essence* of bodies) and denied that these primary qualities have any more reality than taste and odor. His argument for such nonsense was that no one could describe the subject of extension any better than to say it was an extended body, and, as extension cannot be the subject of extension *ad infinitum,* he concluded that the entire universe is an intellectual one. Hylas, who is the materialists' spokesman in Berkeley's *Three Dialogues,* should have given the following answer to Philonous' query concerning the subject of extension. No more is known of the subject of extension than is known of the subject of thought, and so there is no more reason for denying the reality of the one than of the other.[12] Rather than become entangled in such absurdities, we ought to confess that we do not know, and very likely shall never know, the essence of the elemental particles of which all things in nature are composed.[13]

Another insoluble conundrum about matter is the question of its infinity; that is, is there a limit to the extension of matter? The first and fundamental difficulty involved here is the impossibility, Descartes to the contrary, of having a clear idea of infinity. In mathematics, the infinite is cleverly symbolized by a mark resembling a love-knot, but this gives us no clearer understanding of infinity than we had before the invention of the symbol. Like the other meanings of infinity, the mathematical notion simply indicates our inability to come to a termination in numbering. Similarly, the infinitely small is simply that which is smaller than the smallest quantity we can name; fundamentally, the term "infinite" is just another name for one of our incapabilities. For example, when we speak of the infinitely divisible, we are speaking only of our inability to divide a body into parts so small that the parts could not in turn be divided further. As for the infinite extent of the universe, there seems to be no possible answer. If

---

[12] "Corps" (1764), *D.P.,* Naves, pp. 149–51.

[13] *Eléments,* Moland, XXII, 434. In unguarded moments, however, Voltaire writes as if he understood at least something of the essence or nature of matter. In the *Lettres de Memmius à Cicéron* (1771), Moland, XXVIII, 456, for example, when he objects to the doctrine that man has a soul, the argument that he uses is that the essence of the soul would necessarily be always thinking and always feeling, just as matter is always extended and always solid because its essence is to be such.

the universe is bounded, then it is a mere point in relation to un-
bounded space;[14] if it is infinite, its infinity is such that we can
always add to its extent by our imagination. In view, however, of
our inability to form a clear idea of infinity, it is not surprising
that we can give neither an affirmative nor a negative answer to
the question.[15] However, we can argue that matter, if it were
infinite, would have one of the divine attributes;[16] further, the
infinity of matter would make a void impossible, and this would
entail the *necessary* existence of matter, though, again, necessary
existence is an attribute of God, not of creatures.[17]

Where there is question of the *eternity* of matter, Voltaire
seems to be more confident of his ability to give a clearly reasoned answer, though it would seem that "eternity" is just as
difficult to conceive as "infinity." Because there is no more
universally accepted thesis than that from nothing, nothing
comes, it is incomprehensible that matter should have come to be
from nothing. There is also a question here of violating the principle of sufficient reason: if it is not *necessary* for matter to exist,
why should it ever have come to be? But if it exists necessarily,

---

[14] The argument here seems to be that any finite extension, in relation to
infinite extension, would be infinitely less than the infinite extension and so
not extended at all: a point.

[15] "Infini" (1771), *Q.E.*, Moland, XIX, 457. The source of Voltaire's explanation of infinity is most likely John Locke's *Essay on Human Understanding*, especially Book II, c. xvii, paragraphs 7–12 (edited by A. C. Fraser,
2 vols., Oxford: Clarendon Press, 1894, I, 281–85), in which Locke writes of
the infinite divisibility of extension and distinguishes between "infinity of
space" and "space infinite."

[16] It does not seem to bother Voltaire, however, when he asserts that matter is *eternal*, which is also to predicate a divine attribute of it.

[17] "Athée," *D.P.*, Moland, XVII, 457. (Beuchot estimates that this article
was written between 1765 and 1770. See Moland, XVII, viii–ix.) The precise
connection between the impossibility of a void and the necessity of matter
is somewhat obscure, but underlying the argument is very likely the Newtonian reasoning that finite matter and the void require as their ground the
existence of a necessary being. This explanation, however, seems to become
bogged down in a circular argument: Newton proves the existence of God
from the finitude of matter: Voltaire, relying on Newton, proves the finitude of matter from the existence of God. Another possible source of Voltaire's identification of the infinite extension of matter with God is Spinoza's
Ethics, especially Part I, Proposition V (translated by R. H. Elwes, London:
M. W. Dunne Co., 1901), p. 41: "There cannot exist in the universe two or
more substances having the same nature or attribute." The attribute of infinity could not belong both to matter and to God unless one were to assert,
as Spinoza does, that matter is one with the divine substance. It is much more
likely, however, that Voltaire was influenced on this question more by
Newton than by Spinoza.

then it must always have been.[18] The notion that God formed the world from an eternally existing "chaos" is found in all the ancient theogonies, from Hesiod to Philo. To those who hesitate to follow in their footsteps, it may be pointed out that, if the idea of eternal matter is difficult to grasp, it is no more so than that of creation from nothing. The latter notion involves several incomprehensible elements: to create out of nothing would seem to be to change nothing into something.[19] Moreover, there must be some reason for the existence of what exists at the present; but this reason, which is a cause of the existence, must always have been and have been always effective. To think otherwise would be to posit a useless cause existing through all eternity.[20] Worse yet, admitting that matter had a temporal beginning would entail God's existing inactively, and therefore futilely, for the infinite duration preceding the creation of matter.[21] If, however, one deny that matter was produced by God, then matter is necessary and consequently eternal.[22]

As soon as we realize that the whole universe has emanated from God with a sufficient reason, that God must always be active and that, therefore, the universe must have eternally emanated from God, then we are forced to concede that the mat-

---

[18] "Matière" (1764), *D.P.*, Naves, pp. 297–300. It is interesting to note that Voltaire, despite his excoriations of Leibniz, makes use here of Leibniz' principle of sufficient reason. Similarly, while ridiculing the Leibnizian notion of the best-possible world, Voltaire himself explains evil ultimately by positing a God limited in power and, therefore, able to create only the defective world in which we live: the world of *Candide*, which is, for Voltaire too, the best *possible* world.

[19] "Philosophie" (1765), *Nouveaux Mélanges*, Moland, XX, 210–13. Eight years later, Voltaire notes that "Il n'y a jamais eu aucun philosophe, aucun patriarche, aucun homme d'une religion naturelle ou surnaturelle, qui ait enseigné le création du néant." *Fragment d'une lettre sur les dictionnaires satiriques* (1773), Moland, XXIX, 1.

[20] In *Lettres de Memmius à Cicéron* (1771), Moland, XXVIII, 448, Voltaire writes of chaos that it is a mere product of the poetic imagination. Either matter had energy of itself or the energy was in God. If one chooses the first possibility, then one falls into the absurdity of maintaining that chaos, without any design or intelligent plan, gave to itself the movement, the order, and the life that we see in the universe. If one chooses the second possibility, then one must hold that God, the source of energy, *always* gave to matter the orderly motion which it now has; otherwise, one would have to assert that God procrastinated about the work he intended to perform in matter.

[21] "Philosophie," *Nouveaux Mélanges*, Moland, XX, 213.

[22] See also "Infini" (1771), *Q.E.*, Moland, XIX, 455: "The beginning of existing is an absurdity, for nothing can cause a thing to begin existing. From the existence of an atom one must conclude that it has existed eternally."

ter of which all things are formed in also eternal.[23] Or, as Voltaire
puts it in *Le Philosophe ignorant*, he cannot conceive any reason
why matter should have begun to exist at one time rather than at
another. Therefore, he concludes that matter is eternal, and
eternal not as mere chaos, but as matter formed by an eternal
intelligence. The notion of chaos preceding formed matter is
exactly contrary to all the laws of nature; chaos has never had
any existence except in human imaginations. That an active and
necessary being should have been idle, as is implied by the
doctrine of chaos, is unthinkable.[24]

The *Il faut prendre un parti* presents much the same argument.
God, who is necessary, eternal, and essentially active, must have
been acting always, and, Voltaire assumes, such action implies an
effect. Therefore, the world is eternal, just as God is. The intelligent principle of all things cannot act without an antecedent
and necessary reason; because this reason has existed eternally,
the divine activity has gone on eternally, and the universe is
eternal.[25] Voltaire does not give any consideration to medieval
metaphysics, with the meaning it assigns to divine activity, with
its denial that divine activity entails any eternal effect, and with
its extended treatments of the eternity of the divine plan for
temporally finite and contingent beings. Had he studied his
medieval predecessors, it is at least possible that he would not
have been quite so confident of his conclusion regarding the
eternity of matter.

Voltaire observes, however, that Pierre Bayle had argued in
his *Dictionnaire* that matter could not be eternal, that this was

---

[23] *Ibid.*

[24] *Le Philosophe ignorant* (1766), Moland, XXVI, 58–63.

[25] *Il faut prendre un parti* (1772), Moland, XXVIII, 522. A similar argument
is given in the *Dialogues entre Lucrèce et Posidonius* (1756), Moland,
XXIV, 57–58. The Voltairian approach to the problem of an eternal God
causing a universe finite in its duration is one more instance of the general
unawareness among the eighteenth-century thinkers that their medieval
predecessors had grappled with the same problems. St. Thomas, in the
Summa Theologica I, q. 46, a. 1, ad 8, 10, had seen the difficulties which
forced Voltaire to the conclusion that the universe must be eternal. In his
answers to the objections, St. Thomas distinguishes between effects which
follow from the nature, or form, of the agent and effects which follow from
the will of the agent. He concludes: "Ex actione igitur Dei aeterna non
sequitur effectus aeternus sed qualem Deus voluit, ut scilicet haberet esse
post non esse." *Summa Theologica* I, q. 46, a. 1, ad 10; *Opera omnia*, Leonine
edition, IV, 480.

proved by the experiment with the "vial of the four elements." Like so many of the physical experiments of the seventeenth and eighteenth centuries, the experiment involving the vial of the four elements was an extremely simple one, from which, also like so many of the experiments of the period, an unwarranted conclusion was drawn. The experiment consisted in putting into a container some particles of a metal and then, in order, three liquids, each lighter in weight than the preceding chemical. After the vial was shaken, the chemicals were seen to have become mixed so that one could not be distinguished from another. But after some time had elapsed, the four chemicals separated themselves from one another and resumed their original order in the vial. From these facts, Bayle had drawn the conclusion that matter was not eternal. "Chaos" could not have lasted for an eternal length of time, for the elements, no matter how well-mixed, would have separated out, in accordance with their relative heaviness, in some finite length of time. Voltaire refuses to grant Bayle that "chaos" was a mixture of light and heavy things; rather, parts of the chaotic matter became light and heavy and acquired the qualities proper to their species, after God had exercised his causality on them. Therefore, Bayle has not proved the impossibility of matter's being eternal. This, of course, is not to be taken as an admission on Voltaire's part that there ever really was a "chaos," but only that the meaning of "chaos" (as used by those whose poetic imaginations led them to think of it) was not "a complete mixture of elements." [26]

Concerning the motion of matter, Voltaire had a theory drawn almost entirely from Newton. Before expounding his own theory in the *Elements of Newton's Philosophy*, however, the *philosophe* takes a few lines to make short shrift of the Cartesian and Leibnizian theories.[27] Descartes, he says, states *a priori*, without even bothering first to mention the question of force, that there is in the universe a constant quantity of motion. The foundation of this opinion, however, is considerably less obvious than is Descartes' ignorance of the laws of motion. As for Leibniz, though

---

[26] "Ovide" (1756), *Suite des Mélanges*, Moland, XX, 162–64. Not only does Voltaire think it necessary to regard matter as eternal, but he is also of the opinion that it must have had certain properties eternally: shape, inertia, divisibility, and motion. "Matière," *D.P.*, Moland, XX, 51–53.
[27] *Eléments*, Moland, XXII, 435 ff.

he lived in a more enlightened age than did Descartes, he was not able to see that if the same quantity of force existed always, as he granted, then there must also be the same quantity of motion. For force is the cause of motion, and an effect is always proportionate to its cause. Therefore, if the quantity of motion decreases, that of force does also.[28]

Motion is not, as the materialists thought, essential to matter; though the quantity of matter remains the same, the quantity of motion—and so of force—in the universe is constantly changing. It was only because the materialists denied the existence of anything outside matter that they were driven to their conclusion, since for them there was no being to which they could ascribe the causation of a new quantity of motion.[29] Matter, for Voltaire himself, is of itself inert; it receives not only its "form" from God, but also its motion and any increase thereof. To say that God gave to matter at some time in the past its force does not

---

[28] *Ibid.*, p. 437. In *Doutes sur la mesure des forces motrices et sur leur nature* (1741), Moland, XXIII, 171–72, Voltaire lists a number of philosophico-scientific questions concerning force.

[29] *Traité de Métaphysique*, Moland, XXII, 202. The *Traité de Métaphysique* was written for Mme du Châtelet in 1734, reworked over a period of several years, and never published until the Kehl edition of the *Oeuvres complètes* in 1785. Ira O. Wade, in his *Studies on Voltaire* (Princeton: Princeton University Press, 1947), 108–113, observes that subsequent works of Voltaire were much influenced by the fundamental positions Voltaire assumed in the *Traité de Métaphysique* on a number of basic metaphysical problems: the nature of thought and ideogenesis, whether man has a soul, whether there is in man anything immortal, the existence and nature of vice and virtue, and the existence and nature of God. (These, of course, are *metaphysical* problems in the Wolffian sense of metaphysics, not in the Aristotelian or Thomistic sense.) Wade comes to several interesting conclusions regarding the origin and development of the work: it was begun in 1734, under the inspiration of Locke, Clarke, and Malebranche. In December of 1734, Voltaire considered the work finished. At this time it contained only seven of the nine chapters which appear in the Moland text; these seven, according to Wade, included those on the existence and nature of God, on the existence of a human soul, and probably the chapter on free will. In 1735 Voltaire undertook a revision and added two chapters on ethics, Chapters VIII and IX, the result of studying Mandeville's *Essay on the Origin of Moral Virtue*. It was only after the conclusion of the revisions and additions that the treatise was presented to Mme du Châtelet in 1736. However, still further work was done on the book, notably on the section dealing with free will. The philosophical inspiration at this time, according to Wade, stemmed from Christian Wolff and Anthony Collins.

The *Traité de Métaphysique* shall be referred to throughout the remainder of this study as *Traité*.

explain the increases, nor even the decreases, of motion in the universe.[30]

As a result of his admiration for Newton, Voltaire was very much interested in the questions of space and time. In the *Elements of Newton's Philosophy* there is sketched the Newtonian theory of the divine *sensorium*, a theory which seems to have had some considerable attraction for Voltaire, but to have been at the same time slightly more metaphysical than an avowed follower of Locke would like. Newton, Voltaire tells us, thought of space and time as two beings whose existence is a necessary consequence of the existence of God. Because God exists everywhere and for all time, "everywhere" and "all time" must exist too; that is, infinite space and infinite time are real beings, in which material objects have their place and events transpire. While pure space, or a void, is a necessarily existing being, matter exists only by reason of the free choice of the Creator. According to Voltaire's interpretation of Newton, space and time are modes, infinite properties of God; matter is no such thing. If matter were infinite, it would be either God or a property of God, but since it is neither, it is not infinite and could never be infinite. That is, matter is not, as God is, everywhere; there is place or space in which there is no matter.[31]

According to Clarke and Newton, Voltaire says, God is, properly speaking, neither in a place nor in space, neither in time nor in an infinite duration; but because he is necessarily everywhere and necessarily eternal, he constitutes infinite space and infinite time, which are his *sensorium*. This space, which does not in reality have parts, can be conceived of as having different parts, but no one part of space—that, for example, in which Saturn is—can be put in the place of another. Similarly, infinite duration can be thought of as having parts or portions, but no one part of duration can be exchanged with another. When we say that we meas-

---

[30] In "Force physique" (1771), *D.P.*, Moland, XIX, 169, Voltaire defines force as "that weight which one body exercises upon another." In the article, "Influence" (1771), *Q.E.*, Moland, XIX, 462–63, he writes that one ought not admit of any action taking place without physical contact until one has discovered some power capable of acting at a distance, as gravity, for example does. See also on this question, the *Doutes sur la mesure des forces motrices et sur leur nature* (1741), Moland, XXIII, 171–72.

[31] *Exposition du livre des Institutions physiques* (1740), Moland, XXIII, 134–35.

ure space and time we speak improperly, for what we actually measure is bodies extended in space and bodies moving with various velocities.

In all this, there is no indication that Voltaire disagrees with Newton and Clarke on any point at all.[32] However, in the *Philososophical Dictionary* article on "Space," Voltaire states that when he was young he thought he understood the Newtonian doctrine of the divine *sensorium,* but after maturer thought, he was forced to the conclusion that he understood it not at all.[33]

Despite his later disillusionment concerning absolute space and time, Voltaire retained all his life a supreme confidence in his early convictions regarding final causality in the universe. To those who ridiculed the whole concept of final causality by pretending that it entailed believing that noses had been designed for supporting spectacles and fingers for sporting diamond rings, Voltaire rejoined that one must make a distinction between those effects which are always and everywhere invariably the same and the effects which vary. That is, all animals have eyes and see, ears and hear, a mouth and eat, etc.; and in these cases it can be only by perverting the power of thought that one can deny final causality. Where there is question of stones which are not always put together to form a building or noses which do not always function as a support for spectacles, then no final cause is involved. However, even these latter effects, those which are not invariably observed, are included in the plan of God's general providence; nothing happens without this providence, nor contrary to it. Everything which belongs to nature is uniform, unchangeable, the immediate work of the master; he it is who has created the laws by which the ocean ebbs and flows, and the rotary motion of the sun by which this giant star sends its light into the eyes of men and beasts in exactly five and a half minutes. Moreover, if our accomplishments in the arts and crafts are said to be something new, therefore not part of nature, and so not

---

[32] *Eléments*, Moland, XXII, 407–10. With respect to the doctrine of pure space, Voltaire states in a letter to Crown Prince Frederick of Prussia, in 1737, that pure space is extended and that, if Wolff denies pure space, then "We are of two different religions. Let him remain in his and I in mine." *Correspondence*, Besterman, VI, 225.

[33] "Espace" (1771), *Q.E.*, Moland, XIX, 2–3. On the Newtonian concept of space see *The Clarke-Leibniz Correspondence*, edited by H. G. Alexander (Manchester: Manchester University Press, 1956), *passim*, especially pages 5–54.

caused by God, it can be answered that God made man in such wise that man would *necessarily* one day become an artist and a craftsman.

While there is nothing surprisingly profound in these comments Voltaire makes on final causality, they are at least intelligible. The same cannot be said unreservedly, however, for the example given by way of explanation. When he threshes wheat, Voltaire says, the flail is the *final cause* of the separation of the wheat from the chaff. If in threshing his grain he happens to kill the thousands of insects which are in it, this is not by his determined will, but neither is it by chance. It is simply because these insects are there, and *have to be there*, when he threshes his wheat.[34]

In the same place, Voltaire states that he would be willing to admit that final causes are nothing but chimeras, if only he could be convinced that clocks are not made to tell time.[35] When Epicurus and Lucretius deny that eyes are made to see and ears to hear, but then admit that clothes are made to be worn and houses to shelter their inhabitants, then they deny to nature, "the great being, the universal intelligence," what they grant to such lowly people as their tailors and carpenters. It would seem that Epicurus must *deliberately* shut his eyes and his mind to the design that there is in nature. We do not, Voltaire continues, need Homer to tell us that everything in the universe happens according to immutable laws, that everything is arranged, that everything is, in fact, necessary. The thoughtful person can see quite clearly that the world exists by its nature and operates by its own physical laws, or else a supreme being has made it according to his supreme laws. In either case, the laws are unchangeable: heavy bodies always fall toward the center of the earth; pear trees produce only pears; a spaniel acts as a spaniel must instinctively act; an ostrich acts always as an ostrich must necessarily act. Just as it is a contradiction to assert that yesterday was not or that today is non-existent, so it is a contradiction to affirm that that

---

[34] "Fin, Causes finales" (1765), *D.P.*, Naves, pp. 199–201. "Quand nous battons notre blé, le fléau est la cause finale de la separation du grain." The argument is not totally abstruse, but the statement that the final cause is the flail is extremely difficult, if not possible, to reconcile with the ordinary meaning of final cause, as purpose.

[35] *Ibid.*, p. 201. See also the *Q.E.* article of the same title (1770), Naves, pp. 542–43.

which is to come will not inevitably occur. If one could himself change a single insignificant thing in the universe, then that person would be more powerful than God. It is absurd to concede determination in some matters in the universe and deny it in others. However, some men are destined to be absurd; some are destined to reason poorly and others not to reason at all; there are even those destined to persecute those who reason well or poorly.[36]

The determination of every occurrence in the universe is so evidently proved that "chance" is a meaningless word. What men look upon as chance is only an unknown cause of a known effect.[37] To those who insist that there is no need for the hypothesis that God exists and has determined the progress of nature, that the present world is one of the possible arrangements of the material particles of which the universe is formed, Voltaire retorts that they have only one possibility in an unimaginably large number of chance arrangements that the world as it is should have come to be. But that God exists and has determined the world to be as it is, is a proposition resting on innumerable probabilities.[38] In truth, there can be no existent without a reason for its existence, no effect without a cause. This is the first principle of all true philosophy.[39]

While Voltaire was quite satisfied with the certitude of "the principle of sufficient reason," he found himself not nearly so happy with another thesis equally venerable and also popularized by Leibniz, the "principle of continuity." For some time, having been inspired by Newton's view on a "great chain of beings," Voltaire toyed with the notion of such a series of beings ascending from the least perfect material thing to the most perfect substance. Newton believed it was possible that, besides the human soul, there were millions of thinking substances whose nature was absolutely different from man's. Consequently the distinction which has been made between matter and spirit would appear to be like the definition a blind and deaf man would give of the senses, suspecting the existence neither of sight nor hear-

---

[36] "Destin" (1764), *D.P.*, Naves, pp. 164–66.

[37] "Atomes" (1770), *Q.E.*, Moland, XVII, 478.

[38] Letter to M. le Marquis de Villevielle, August 26, 1768, Moland, XLVI, 104–05: "Il y a un nombre innombrable de probabilités qu'il existe un Dieu formateur, et vous n'avez, messieurs, tout au plus que l'unité pour vous: jugez donc, si la chance n'est pas pour moi."

[39] *Lettres de Memmius à Cicéron* (1771), Moland, XXVIII, 441.

ing. "By what right can you say that God has not filled space with an infinity of substances which have nothing in common with man?" Voltaire asks in the *Elements of Newton's Philosophy*.[40]

However, about thirty years later, Voltaire writes that he can no longer accept with his former admiration what he regarded as the Platonic theory of a chain of beings rising from the most insignificant atom to the supreme being. It is the imagination which suggests that there is an imperceptible transition from gross matter to organized matter, from plants to zoophytes, from zoophytes to animals, from animals to men, from men to genies, from genies with an aethereal body to immaterial substances, and finally, through a thousand different orders of such substances, to God himself. In reality, there is not even such a gradation in the plant and animal kingdom; that is, some species of plants and animals have become extinct, and it is even probable that there have been races of men which will never be found again. Further, there is a visible gap between the monkey and man. One could imagine a featherless biped which would be intelligent but without the ability to speak, which would react to man's signs and would serve him; but such a creature, though a grade higher than a monkey and lower than a man, does not exist in reality. If there is any great chain which binds the entire universe together, it is certainly the force of gravity discovered by Newton, and not any chimerical gradation of perfection.[41]

Not only is there no absolutely gradual transition from one kind of being to another, but there is also a definite cleavage between living and nonliving things. For Voltaire, things can be said to be alive if they have the faculty of sensation. "Life is organization with the faculty of sensation."[42] Life cannot be attributed properly to plants; it is only by way of metaphor and catachresis that one can refer to plants as living. They are organized and they carry on vegetative activities, but they lack the essential characteristic of life: they do not sense. Not only is the power of sensation the distinguishing feature of living things, but it may also serve to define man more accurately than does the power of

[40] *Eléments*, Moland, XXII, 423.

[41] "Chain des êtres créés" (1764), *D.P.*, Naves, pp. 101–02. See also Arthur O. Lovejoy, *The Great Chain of Being* (Cambridge: Harvard University Press, 1933), pp. 252–53.

[42] "Vie" (1772), *Q.E.*, Moland, XX, 578: "La vie est organization avec capacité de sentir."

thinking. That is, idiots, who do not have any ideas at all, but certainly are sentient, are so far from being nonhuman that they can generate human beings.[43]

It will be seen from the foregoing, then, that Voltaire's "philosophy of nature," or "cosmology," is a somewhat naive eclecticism compounded of pre-Socratic atomism, not-too-perspicacious common sense, scientific empiricism, Newtonian physics, and Lockean skepticism concerning the possibility of man's knowledge transcending the immediately sensible. Of particular note are the conclusions that matter is eternal, that because matter is not necessary it is not infinite in extension, that matter is of itself inert, that motion is not an essential property of matter, that there are increases and decreases in the quantity of motion and force in the universe, that the various elemental particles of matter are immutable because they are perfectly solid, and that whatever occurs in nature occurs necessarily, for a sufficient reason, and with a final cause.

Having considered Voltaire's views on the material universe in general, we can proceed to an examination of that most interesting part of the universe, man himself, and attempt to ascertain whether the *philosophe's* position on this question has any important consequences on the focal problem of the relationship existing between God and the universe.

---

[43] *Ibid.*, pp. 578–79. Had Voltaire made a more thorough study of St. Thomas, the *philosophe* might have seen a way to reconcile the absence of ideas in idiots with their human nature, without making sentiency the distinguishing feature of human nature. In the *Summa Theologica* I, q. 85, aa. 1 and 2, St. Thomas explains his theory of the part that sensation plays in intellection. According to this Thomistic theory, it is precisely in the area of sentiency and its organic basis that the idiot is defective, for the exercise of the intellect depends upon the preparatory work done by means of the senses. The idiot, then, has the power of intellect, but is impeded in its exercise. *Opera Omnia*, Leonine edition, V, 330–35.

CHAPTER THREE

Man

DESPITE HIS PARTICIPATION in the eighteenth century's enthusiasm for natural science, Voltaire retained a sufficiently humanistic frame of mind to be much more interested in the nature of man *as man* than in man as merely a physical part of the material universe. Just as in his considerations of the material universe, Voltaire had asked the traditional questions, so in his study of man, he proposes the same problems that had intrigued philosophers for centuries: whether man has a nature specifically different from that of brutes, how man acquires his ideas, how he compares and arranges the ideas he has acquired, whether his ideas correspond to an extra-mental reality, whether man has a soul or whether matter itself can think, what are the limits of human knowledge, and whether there is any survival after death. These traditional questions, then, with Voltaire's somewhat untraditional answers, will form the subject matter of this chapter. While it may seem that most of these questions have only a remote connection with deism as a theory of the relationship existing between God and the universe, the answers which are given to them are fundamental in solving the problems of human freedom and human ability to know God. And these latter problems have consequences which are in the strictest sense elements of Voltaire's deism.

In the *Treatise on Metaphysics* one can find Voltaire's earliest extended writing on the question of man's nature. He claims that certain previous writers made pronouncements on this problem without having bothered to observe man carefully as he actually is and, consequently, have produced such absurdities as Malebranche's theory that man is a soul more closely united with God than with its body, a soul that sees and thinks everything in God. The true *philosophe*, however, will use the disinterested, scientific method. That is, Voltaire proposes to adopt the attitude of a nonhuman but intelligent being descended from the planet Mars or Jupiter, devoid of all prejudices of education, country, and philosophy. This, he assures the reader, is at least as easy as imagining himself in the sun for the purpose of seeing the true order of planetary motions, rather than the merely apparent order which the planets exhibit as seen from the earth. Having imagined himself in the rôle of interplanetary visitor, he will be able to make a synoptic observation of man as he exists in all countries and all centuries.[1]

The first stop of this Martian visitor is the country of the Kafirs in South Africa, where he observes monkeys, elephants, lions, and a Negro infant. All give some evidence of thinking, for all seem to have some sort of language and all appear to direct their activities toward a definite end. Which of these, he asks himself, is the most intelligent and, therefore, a man rather than a beast? At first it seems that the child is least self-sufficient and least able to make its wants known. However, after some time, the child has acquired a larger store of ideas than the monkeys, elephants, and lions; he has a richer language and, despite his lesser degree of strength, he appears to be the superior. In view of this, the Martian can only conclude that this child is a man rather than a beast. Consequently, he forms a definition of man: a man is a black animal, having wool on its head, walking on two feet, almost as adroit as a monkey, less strong than other animals of similar size, equipped with more ideas than they have and with a greater facility for expressing them. He is subject to the same necessities as the others, for he is born, lives for a time, and dies, just as they do.[2]

This definition, however, is not able to withstand the introduction of additional evidence: a trip to the East Indies reveals that, while the monkeys, elephants, and lions there are like those in Africa, the men are different; they are yellow, have black curls instead of wool on their heads, and, most astonishing of all, they think differently on all subjects from the way the Negroes of

---

[1] *Traité*, Moland, XXII, 190–91.

[2] *Ibid.*, pp. 191–92. Voltaire entitles this chapter of the *Traité*, "Des différentes espèces d'hommes," and he regards the African Negro and the French white man as being as different from one another as two biological species. See, however, the article, "Bêtes" (1764), *D.P.*, Naves, pp. 50–53, for Voltaire's theory that the distinction between the brute and human souls, that is, between brute and human faculties of sensation and thought, is only one of degree.

Africa think. Moreover, trips to other parts of the earth reveal that there are still other species of men, some with yellow hair and white skins, some with long beards, some with no beards at all. The most peculiar species of the lot, however, is found in Goa: a man in a long black soutane, one who says that it is his office to instruct others. Part of his instruction is the information that all these various species of men have descended from a single pair of parents. This the Martian visitor is unable to accept, for it seems to him that expecting one species of man to give rise to another is like expecting a pear tree to yield something other than pears.[3]

Having said this much, Voltaire abandons the rôle of Martian empiricist, inserts a chapter on the existence of God, and proceeds to examine the process whereby man acquires his ideas. The method of investigation, while no longer Martian, is nonetheless still empirical. One must not, Voltaire says, formulate ingenious hypotheses by which one hopes to explain everything; rather, one must begin by an exact analysis of things and then, with great caution, attempt to see whether the analysis reveals any principles in view of which a relationship can be posited among the things observed.[4]

It is precisely the failure to proceed in this manner that has led certain persons to maintain that all men have a store of metaphysical ideas, including the ideas of the infinitude and immensity of God. If these innatists had taken the trouble to make some observations, they would have learned that there are thousands of men who have not the slightest notion of these things, and that an infant has none of these ideas at all until they are given to him,

---

[3] *Traité*, Moland, XXII, 192. Almost thirty years later, in the introduction to the *Essai sur les moeurs et l'esprit des nations* (1765), Moland, XI, 7, Voltaire is willing to admit the possibility of a species of satyrs having risen from crossbreeding humans and horses, a species, however, which would not be able to reproduce itself, just as a mule, a result of crossbreeding, is sterile. "Il est parlé de satyres dans presque tous les auteurs anciens. Je ne vois pas que leur existence soit impossible; on étouffe encore en Calabre quelques monstres mis au monde par les femmes. Il n'est pas improbable que dans les pays chauds des singes aient subjugué des filles. . . . Il faut donc que ces accouplements aient été communs; et jusqu'à ce qu'on soit mieux éclairci, il est à présumer que des espèces monstrueuses ont pu naître de ces amours abominables." Voltaire, of course, has no right to call them *amours abominables*, if he really meant what he said about the necessity of the various species, whether formed immediately by God or through the infallible operations of the laws divinely imposed on creatures.

[4] *Traité*, Moland, XXII, 203.

and even then the ideas are very imperfect and purely negative. If there is anything that can be truly demonstrated outside mathematics, then it is the fact that men do not have any innate ideas. If they had, all men would be born with an idea of God, all would have the same idea of him, and all would share the same metaphysical notions. It is, therefore, beyond the possibility of doubt that our first ideas are our sensations.[5] Little by little, man receives composite ideas from what has impinged upon the sense organs; the memory retains these perceptions; finally, man arranges his collections of perceptions under certain general ideas. It is from this faculty of composing and arranging the various perceptions under general ideas that there results all the vast knowledge of mankind.[6]

To those who object that ideas of the infinite in duration or in extent or in number could not be formed from perceptions, it must be answered that, if they look within themselves, objectors will find that they have no complete or even positive idea of infinity. They have simply become aware of the impossibility of counting to the point beyond which one could no longer count. It is this inability which they call "infinite"; "infinite" is a name for human ignorance, not for an idea that exceeds the sense powers. The fact that mathematicians talk about infinity is no more a proof that man has an idea of infinity than the fact that man can demonstrate the existence of God is a proof that man has an idea of God.[7] If one asks, then, *how* our ideas come from our senses, it can only be said that, until man becomes of another nature and acquires other organs which will enable him to perceive his own substance and the essence of his own ideas, one can only say that this is a secret of the Creator. As man is presently constituted, he may as well wish to fly as to understand how he senses. Nevertheless, one can be certain that ideas do come from the senses, for where there is a sense lacking, there are also lacking the ideas belonging to the sense. If one attempts to go beyond this fact, then one is attempting to exceed the limits of human reason. The true philosopher is one who knows how far to go in

---

[5] *Ibid.*, p. 203: "Il est donc indubitable que nos premières idées sont nos sensations."

[6] *Ibid.*

[7] *Ibid.*, p. 204. See also John Locke, *Essay Concerning Human Understanding*, II, xvii, 3, "How we come by the idea of infinity" (Fraser, I, 278).

his search and when to stop; he forges ahead only when he has a dependable guide.[8]

Despite his own warning that man cannot understand anything about the manner in which he senses, Voltaire makes it quite evident in his later writings that he is convinced that ideas come from the senses. All antiquity, he asserts, maintained that there is nothing in our understanding which was not first in the senses.[9] It took Descartes and his "romances" to assert that even metaphysical ideas are innate, a doctrine rejected by the faculty of theology at the Sorbonne because the idea was new, and then accepted later by the same faculty because Locke, an Englishman, had proved Descartes' theory was impossible. However, no matter how many faculties of theology make pronouncements on the subject, all philosophers will see that ideas begin in sensation and that memory is merely a continued sensation. A man deprived of all senses would, if he could live in such a state, be also deprived of all ideas. Even metaphysical notions come only through the senses, for no one can have even an imperfect idea of infinity unless he has sensed certain boundaries and the removal of those boundaries. As for Descartes' theory that the soul resides in the pineal gland, there is no evidence, says Voltaire, that anyone can solve a geometrical problem once his head is cut off, even though the pineal gland remains unchanged for a long time afterwards.[10]

With respect to the question of the mechanism involved in ideogenesis, Voltaire is invincibly certain that his first ideas and sensations have come to him in spite of himself. He sees quite clearly that he cannot be the source of his own ideas, that he cannot give himself anything, that he has received everything. Nor can the material objects about him give him sensations or ideas, for it is not possible that a bit of matter should be able to produce

---

[8] *Traité*, Moland, XXII, 205.

[9] This is a fairly good example of Voltaire's carelessness in making statements about the history of philosophy. As a matter of fact, the more common opinion of "antiquity" was that ideas could not possibly come from the senses, because the soul could not be affected by the body, which was inferior to it. This was the position of Platonists in the ancient period and Augustinians in the medieval.

[10] "Sensations" (1764), *D.P.*, Naves, pp. 391–92. Descartes, of course, did not teach that the soul "resided" in the pineal gland, although it had its "seat" there chiefly.

a thought in him.[11] It is God who does all, produces everything in him. One should not, however, blame God for the errors of one's senses; the unchanging laws of nature, which have their source in the immutable will of God, are adapted to our senses and cannot produce errors. We see, not things themselves, but only the appearances of things. Therefore, if the sun appears to us to be flat and two feet in diameter, then that is the way it *appears*. It is the understanding which must go on to interpret the appearances and come to a knowledge of the thing as it really is.[12] Each of man's senses performs the function for which nature has designed it. They work together to convey to the mind, by means of experience, the degree of knowledge attainable by our nature. If we expect our eyes to reveal to us the solidity, size, and distance of objects, we are asking of them a function for which they were not made; the sense of touch and experience are necessary for the knowledge of such qualities.[13]

Though he was not certain of the notion, Voltaire suggested a theory that it was the imagination which was the sole instrument for retaining simple impressions and for putting simple ideas together to form complex and general ideas. In view of the former function, the imagination can be called "passive"; it requires no help from the will, whether one is awake or asleep, but it is an internal sense which operates necessarily, representing what our eyes have seen, our ears heard, our fingers touched. Now, if such ideas are reproduced in us independently of our will when we are asleep, is it not possible, Voltaire asks, that our waking ideas are no more dependent upon us? If Malebranche had been satisfied with saying only that our ideas are given us by God, could anyone have opposed him? [14]

---

[11] "Idée" (1771), *Q.E.*, Naves, p. 556.

[12] "Ciel matériel" (1770), *Q.E.*, Moland, XVIII, 184–85.

[13] "Distance" (1771), *Q.E.*, Moland, XVIII, 408. Voltaire had come to this conclusion largely through the report of a man who was enabled by surgery to see for the first time and who, in describing his first visual sensations, made it clear that solidity, size, and distance were not given by sight except in cooperation with the experiences of touch. This is almost certainly the same man referred to by Locke in his *Essay*, II, ix, 8 (Fraser, I, 186–87).

[14] "Imagination" (1765), *Nouveaux Mélanges*, Moland, XIX, 429. Ralph W. Church, in *A Study of the Philosophy of Malebranche* (London: George Allen and Unwin, 1931), pp. 116–42, gives a valuable explanation of Malebranche's theory of sense and imagination, as opposed to true knowledge in the "vision of God." See also Malebranche, *De la recherche de la vérité* (2 vols., ed. M. F. Bouillier, Paris: Garnier, 1893), I, 326–35, for the meaning of Malebranche's statement that man receives all his knowledge from God.

The imagination has another function also: it is the source of all man's passions and errors. In fact, rather than say that the functioning of the imagination depends upon the will, we must admit that the will is determined by the ideas produced by the imagination. It is the imagination alone which produces fear, the desire for glory, and the enthusiasm of fanatics. But of how the passive imagination operates, we know no more than we do of other operations in nature.[15]

The active imagination is the faculty of joining and separating ideas; while it appears to create, it merely rearranges the impressions which are retained by the passive imagination. Man does not create ideas; he only modifies the ideas he receives necessarily. While it may seem that the active imagination is dependent upon the will, a more careful analysis will show that it is every bit as independent of voluntary control as is the passive imagination. If, for example, one were to ask a hundred people to imagine a certain kind of new machine, ninety-nine of them would have no image of it at all, no matter how hard they tried. The hundredth enjoys a special gift which is called "genius," something which we recognize as inspired and divine. No one creates a single image or ideas; we only collect and combine them. And even abstract ideas are only the effect of this imagination. "Triangle" has no meaning aside from some at least confused image of a particular triangle; the units with which one counts have meaning only if the imagination represents them as discrete extended bodies. "Truth" is significant only because one has had experience of having been told certain things existed and then of perceiving by the senses the existence of those things.[16]

Peculiarly enough, some philosophers, such as Berkeley, who have had the hardihood to extend their investigations beyond what is received by the senses and preserved by the imagination have also, says Voltaire, been the same men who doubt what is extraordinarily clear. That is, these men, after pretending to explain the essence of man and the process whereby he obtains his ideas, are inexplicably skeptical enough to ask whether the things of which man has ideas are really objects outside man. This question arises because men are deceived when they think the things they perceive in dreams are real, and because the senses often lead them to perceive things otherwise than those things really are. If

[15] "Imagination," *loc. cit.*, pp. 430–31.
[16] *Ibid.*, p. 428.

one can be deceived sometimes, why not always? To the first argument, Voltaire objects that even the perceptions one has in dreams are the result of remembered sense experiences. Moreover, if one perceives that he is struck by a stone, it would be unreasonable to imagine that his memory has caused the broken bone that ensues, and so he can scarcely entertain the notion that he is merely dreaming of being struck by the stone. As for our senses deceiving us, while it is true that we may be deceived about colors and sounds, we cannot be deceived about the extension or impenetrability of objects, for the last two qualities are of the essence of matter.[17] Therefore, we cannot be deceived about the real existence of the objects of our knowledge.[18]

While Voltaire is quite serious about this argument, he also twits the skeptics a bit in asking what difference it would make in their conduct if the objects of their knowledge did not really exist. The difference, he answers for them, would consist only in saying, instead of "There was a battle in which ten thousand men were killed; an officer broke his leg, and the surgeon cut it off," "There appeared to be a battle; an officer appeared to break his leg, and the surgeon appeared to cut it off." [19]

In a letter to Jean Baptiste Nicolas Formont, written in 1733, Voltaire also ridicules Malebranche's theory about the certitude of man's knowledge of material objects outside himself. That "sublime fool," he says, holds that man cannot know with certitude of the existence of bodies unless he knows it by faith; yet, this same fool will not grant that spiritual substances cannot be known except by faith! Malebranche, Descartes, and others of like mind have been fooled in this matter because it is a fact that men are much more certain of the truth of their feelings, of their thoughts, than of the existence of material objects. Nevertheless, the fact that one is certain that he is thinking is not sufficient to warrant the assertion that man is anything other than thinking matter.[20]

Man is, Voltaire is satisfied, sufficiently sure that he senses, that

---

[17] This despite Voltaire's frequent statements that we do not know, and cannot know, the essence of matter.

[18] *Traité*, c. iv, "Qu'il y a en effet des objets extérieurs," Moland, XXII, 206–08.

[19] *Ibid*., pp. 206–07.

[20] Letter of July 26, 1773, *Correspondence*, Besterman, III, 111. Jean Baptiste Nicolas Formont was a literary dilettante, befriended by Voltaire. Formont died in 1758.

he is material, and that the objects of his knowledge really exist outside himself. But there remains the question of whether, over and above his material body, man has a soul. For solving this problem, Voltaire says, he must become again that nonhuman, intelligent being descended from another planet, unprejudiced and disinterested. Even then, it would be only if he were a superior sort of being to whom the Creator had revealed his secrets that he would be able, by observing man, to say exactly what a human being is. But, since he must confess that he is not that superior sort of being, he must be content with the method which is available to one of his intellectual blindness: careful analysis proceeding from one part to another, until some judgment may be made about the whole. He imagines, then, that this interplanetary visitor arrives in Africa and finds that the Hottentots have the same sort of physical organs and operations as the other animals; they have the same passions, the same needs, and they all express themselves in their own language. It is, in fact, the language of the brute animals which the traveler would understand, for each expression in such a language has a necessary and sensible relation to its object; the sounds and movements by which an animal expresses hunger or pain from a wound are such that they are naturally related to their objects. Though this language is quite limited, that is to be expected, inasmuch as such animals have very few ideas.[21]

The Hottentots, on the contrary, have certain ideas and certain combinations of ideas which are lacking in the brutes, and the Hottentots express these ideas by a differently articulated language. The more the investigator examines the brutes and the Hottentots, the more he is impelled to think that they are "different species of the same genus." This means, for Voltaire, that both men and brute animals have the ability to retain ideas, both have dreams made up of faint images of what they have experienced during their waking hours.[22] Both have a faculty of

---

[21] *Traité*, c. v, "Si l'homme a une âme, et ce que ce peut être," Moland, XXII, 210 ff.

[22] It would seem that Voltaire is violating, in at least a venial manner, the ethics of empiricism when he purports to relate what occurs in the dreams of brute animals; moreover, his scientific method leaves something to be desired when he writes about Hottentots, East Indians, and American Indians, none of whom he had observed in their own countries and about whom he had only the most contradictory reports at his disposal in the writings of various world travelers.

sensing which grows with their physical organs, becomes weakened as the organs are weakened, and perishes when the organs perish. That is, the difference is one of degree; men are merely capable of having more ideas than do brutes, not of performing any activities entirely lacking in brutes. Therefore, if one wishes to insist that men have a soul because they give evidence of thinking, then one must grant that brute animals have souls too, a concession which Voltaire seems to assume no proponent of the theory of human souls would want to make. Therefore, one must reject the notion of a soul as the source of ideas and sensations and look elsewhere.[23]

The first guess of the visitor from outer space would be that, since life, sensation, and thought do not come from the nature of matter, of which animal bodies are formed, it must be God who has given to these bodies the power of sensing and of having ideas in the various degrees appropriate for their diverse physical structures. Finding that there are other men who exceed the sensing and thinking capacities of the Hottentots just as the Hottentots exceed those of the monkey, the investigator is even more inclined to the view that the difference between one animal and another, including men, is only one of degree.[24]

Certain philosophers, however, approach the visiting empiricist and explain to him that he is mistaken; man is entirely different from the other animals; he has a spiritual and immortal soul. This, they reason, is necessarily true, for if thought were merely something composed of matter, it would have to have the properties of matter; it would have to be divisible and capable of motion. But since thought is not divisible, and not made up of physical parts, it must be simple and immortal, a divine work. To this, the celestial visitor answers that it must follow then that all animals have such a soul, for all have the same sense organs as those which man uses in thinking; otherwise one would be maintaining that God has given to brute animals organs which are useless. If one is not willing to grant a spiritual, immortal soul to a flea, then one must not grant it to man. All that can be known with

---

[23] *Traité*, Moland, XXII, 210.

[24] Voltaire's failure even to consider the possibility of animals having souls can perhaps be explained by the fact that, though he was not a Cartesian, yet he had imbibed much of the Cartesian spirit in spite of himself. Therefore, the Cartesian dichotomy between soul and immaterial being on the one hand, and body and material being on the other, seems to have been accepted by Voltaire without any realization of its source.

certitude is that there is something common between the animals called "men" and the animals called "brutes." [25]

Though the philosophers who are anxious to explain the nature of the soul assure the visitor to earth that matter cannot think, he cannot see that this is impossible. If thought were something composed of matter, then he would be willing to grant that it ought to be extended and divisible; but, if thought is an *attribute* given by God to matter, then such would not necessarily follow. God has, in fact, communicated to matter other properties which are not extended or divisible. Gravitation, for example, whose cause is known no more than that of thought, has been demonstrated to be real, though it is nothing extended or divisible. Moreover, in nature, like effects must have like causes. Thus, if thought differs in men and beasts only by degree, then its cause must be the same: an attribute given by God to matter. Even if one were to grant the existence of an immaterial soul, one could scarcely say what this would be, unless one defined it as thought; but no one can reasonably hold that man is always thinking. Therefore, this will not do. The only reasonable solution, Voltaire says, is to admit that God has organized the parts of bodies in such a way as to make them capable of thinking, just as he has organized the parts in such a way that they are capable of eating and digesting food.[26]

---

[25] *Traité*, Moland, XXII, 211. See also the *Lettres de Memmius à Cicéron*, Moland, XXVIII, 459: "Les animaux ont les mêmes facultés que nous. Organisés, comme nous, ils reçoivent comme nous la vie, ils la donnent de même. Ils commencent comme nous le mouvement, et le communiquent. Ils ont des sens et des sensations, des idées, de la mémoire. Quel est l'homme assez fou pour penser que le principe de toutes ces choses est un principe inétendu? Nul mortel n'a jamais osé proférer cette absurdité. Pourquoi donc serions-nous insensés pour imaginer cet esprit en faveur de l'homme?"

[26] *Traité*, Moland, XXII, 212. An obvious source of Voltaire's position concerning thinking matter is John Locke's *Essay Concerning Human Understanding*, IV, iii, 6 (Fraser edition, II, 192–93). "We have the ideas of *matter* and *thinking*, but possibly shall never know whether any mere material being thinks or no. . . . For I see no contradiction in it, that the first Eternal thinking Being, or Omnipotent Spirit, should, if he pleased, give to certain systems of created senseless matter, put together as he thinks fit, some degrees of sense, perception, and thought. . . ." In answer to the objections of Edward Stillingfleet, Bishop of Worcester, Locke wrote, "The general idea of substance being the same everywhere, the modification of thinking, or the power of thinking, joined to it, makes it a spirit, without considering what other modifications it has, or whether it has the modifications of solidity or not. As, on the other side, substance, that has the modification of solidity, is matter, whether it has the modification of thinking or not. And

In the *Lettres de Memmius à Cicéron* the argument is considerably expanded. If one says that the soul is an unknown substance whose essence it is to think and to feel, part of the statement can be granted; namely, that the soul is unknown.

> But that it is a substance—this I deny. If it were a substance, its essence would be to feel and to think, as the essence of matter is extension and solidity. Then the soul would be feeling and thinking always, just as matter is always extended and solid. However, it is quite certain that we neither feel nor think all the time. One would have to be opinionated to a ridiculous degree to maintain that one has sensations or ideas in a profound, dreamless sleep. It is, then, a creation of the mind,[27] a chimera, a would-be substance that would lose its essence for half its lifetime.[28]

Our sensations, ideas, acts of willing, etc., do not come from a soul; they are given to the body by the supreme intelligence which animates all nature. Man has the power of thinking, without being essentially thought, or soul, just as man has the power of moving, without being movement.[29]

In his correspondence, Voltaire frequently brought up the question of whether God could give to matter the power of thinking or whether, to account for the fact that man thinks, one must posit an immaterial substance, a soul. In a letter to Jean

---

therefore, if your lordship means by a 'spiritual,' an immaterial substance, I grant I have not proved, nor upon my principles can it be proved . . . that there is an immaterial substance in us that thinks." *Locke's Philosophical Works* (2 vols., London: Bell, 1875), Appendix, "Controversy with the Bishop of Worcester," II, 387.

[27] Voltaire writes that the soul is an *être de raison,* but he scarcely means exactly what the scholastics meant by *ens rationis.*

[28] *Lettres de Memmius à Cicéron* (1771), Moland, XXVIII, 456: "Mais substance, je le nie. Si elle était substance, son essence serait de sentir et de penser, comme celle de la matière est l'étendue et la solidité. Alors l'âme sentirait toujours et penserait toujours, comme la matière est toujours étendue. Cependant il est très-certain que nous ne sentons ni ne pensons toujours. Il faut être d'une opiniâtreté ridicule pour soutenir que, dans un profond sommeil, quand on ne rêve point, on a du sentiment et des idées. C'est donc un être de raison, une chimère, qu'une prétendue substance qui perdrait son essence pendant la moitié de sa vie." Some present-day psychologists, with their theory that there is no such thing as dreamless sleep and no such thing as a state in which there is absolutely no perception whatsoever, would scarcely regard this argument as valid. See, for instance, Donald M. Johnson, *Essentials of Psychology* (New York: McGraw-Hill, 1948), p. 99.

[29] *Lettres de Memmius à Cicéron, loc. cit.,* p. 457. See also, *L'A.B.C.* (1762), Moland, XXVII, 327–330.

Baptiste Nicolas Formont, during the period in which Voltaire was becoming acquainted with the teaching of Locke, Voltaire wrote:

> It is true that we can understand neither how matter thinks nor how a thinking being is united with matter. But of the two equally incomprehensible things, one must be true, just as with the divisibility or indivisibility of matter it is necessary that one be true, though neither is understandable. And so with the eternity and creation of matter; while both are unintelligible, one must be true.[30]
>
> In order to know whether matter thinks, we have no fixed rule which will lead us to a demonstration as in geometry. . . . But we have the probabilities; it is a question, therefore, of knowing which is more probable. The most reasonable axiom in the field of physics is that *the same effects must be attributed to the same cause.* Now, the same effects are seen in beasts and in men; therefore, the same cause animates them. The beasts sense and think to a certain extent; they have ideas. Man has, over and above this, a greater combination of ideas, a much greater store of them. But a difference of degree does not make a difference of species. . . .
>
> Thought and feeling are not essential to matter, doubtless, as is impenetrability. Motion, gravitation, vegetative powers, and life are not essential to matter, and no one would imagine these qualities to be in matter if he had not been convinced by experience.
>
> It is therefore very probable that nature has given thoughts to brains as it has given vegetative life to trees; it is very probable that we think with our brain just as we walk with our feet.[31]

---

[30] In this context Voltaire is using "creation" in a relatively traditional sense, rather than in the sense he later came to adopt. Voltaire's later notion of "creation" is that it is simply the formation, by the divine being, of the universe from eternally existing matter. In the latter sense there is no contradiction between "creation" and eternally existing matter.

[31] Letter of December 13, 1735, *Correspondence*, Besterman, IV, 207: "Il est vrai que nous ne pouvons comprendre ni comment la matière pense, ni comment un être pensant est uni à la matière. Mais de ces deux choses également incompréhensibles, il faut que l'une soit vraie, comme de la divisibilité ou de l'indivisibilité de la matière, il faut que l'une ou l'autre soit, quoique ni l'une ni l'autre ne soit compréhensible. Ainsi, la création et l'éternité de la matière sont inintelligibles, et cependant il faut que l'une des deux soit admise.

Pour savoir si la matière pense ou non, nous n'avons point de règle fixé qui nous puisse conduire à une démonstration, comme en géométrie . . . Mais nous avons des probabilités; il s'agit donc de savoir ce qui est le plus probable. L'axiome le plus raisonnable en fait de physique est celui-ci: *les mêmes effets doivent être attribué à la même cause.* Or, les mêmes effets se voient dans les bêtes et dans les hommes; donc la même cause les anime. Les bêtes sentent et pensent à un certain point; elles ont les idées; les hommes

In the following year, 1736, Voltaire is discussing the same question with the same correspondent:

> It is true that, if it could be proved that there is an incompatibility and a formal contradiction between matter and thought, all the probabilities in favor of thinking matter would be destroyed.
>
> It is true, therefore, that the brunt of the argument, as you say so well, is borne by this question: *Is thinking matter a contradiction?*
>
> 1. I shall observe that it is not a question of knowing whether matter thinks by itself; matter does nothing; it can have neither motion nor existence by itself (at least that much appears to me to be demonstrated). It is a question solely of knowing if the creator, who has given to matter both motion and the incomprehensible power of communicating it, could also give thought to matter, unite it with matter.
>
> Now, if it were true that it had been proved that God could not communicate thought to matter or unite it with matter, then it would seem to me that it would be proved also by that fact that God could not unite a thinking being with matter; for I would make the same objections to a thinking being united with matter as are made against thought united with matter.[32]

That is, if Voltaire is wrong in asserting that God could give thoughts to matter, then people such as Descartes and Malebranche would be equally wrong in asserting that God has given

---

n'ont au dessus d'elles qu'une plus grande combinaison d'idées, un plus grand magasin. Le plus et le moins ne changent point l'espèce. . . .

La pensée et le sentiment ne sont pas essentiels, sans doute, à la matière, comme l'impénétrabilité. Mais le mouvement, la gravitation, la végétation, la vie, ne lui sont pas essentielles, et personne n'imaginerait ces qualités dans la matière, si on ne s'en était pas convaincu par l'expérience.

Il est donc très probable que la nature a donné des pensées à des cerveaux, comme la végétation à les arbres, que nous pensons par le cerveau, de même que nous marchons avec le pied."

[32] Letter of c. January 15, *Correspondence*, Besterman, V, 18–20: "Il est vrai que si l'on peut prouver qu'il a une incompatibilité, une contradiction formelle entre la matière & la pensée, toutes les probabilités en faveur de la matière pensante sont détruites.

Il est donc vrai que la fort de la dispute, comme vous le dites très bien, roule sur cette question: *La matière pensante est elle une contradiction?*

1. J'observerai qu'il ne s'agit pas de savoir si la matière pense par elle même; elle ne fait rien, elle ne peut avoir le mouvement ni l'existence par elle même; (du moins cela me paraît démontré) il s'agit uniquement de savoir si le créateur qui lui a donné le mouvement, le pouvoir incompréhensible de le communiquer, peut aussi lui communiquer, lui unir la pensée.

Or s'il était vrai qu'on prouvât que dieu n'a pu communiquer, n'a pu unir la pensée à la matière, il me paraît qu'on prouverait aussi par là que dieu n'a pu lui unir un être pensant; car je dirai contre l'être pensant uni à la matière tout ce qu'on dira contre la pensée unie à la matière."

to matter a soul whose essence it is to think. If thought and matter are contradictories, a thinking soul could not be united to a material body.[33]

In another place, while writing on the subject of "Ideas," Voltaire declares that he does not know a single syllable about how man thinks, that God has not shared his secret about the matter with anyone. If man is completely ignorant of how his heart beats, of how his blood flows through his veins, of how he is able to move his limbs, then it is not strange that he does not understand how he feels and how he thinks.[34] Further, those who imagine that the faculty of thinking, of whose mechanism they are ignorant, makes a man more noble than the sun or other material things, are stating something which is not proved. This is not for man to judge, for it is not proper that one who has an interest in a case should hand down the decision. Commonly, we say that one thing is superior to another if the first has required more work on the part of the maker, but no one can say that it took a greater effort on the part of God to create a five-foot animal that thinks indifferently well then to create the sun. Moreover, the sun is much more useful to the world than any man, for the whole material world depends upon it. And who would suggest that a few ideas received into a brain are worth more than the universe? [35]

---

[33] See also the article, "Homme" (1771), *Q.E.*, Moland, XIX, 384–85: "If, as Pascal says, thought is that which makes man to be man, then thought would be his essence, as extension and solidity are the essence of matter. Man would think essentially and at all times, just as matter is always extended and solid . . . If thought were essential to man, then God could not deprive him of his understanding . . . man would then be God, for, if one is to define God at all, one should define him as the being whose essence and existence are thought . . . Moreover, thought is sometimes feeble, sometimes vigorous, sometimes reasonable, sometimes absurd . . . essence is something quite different; it never changes; it admits of no increase or diminution."

[34] "Idée" (1765), *D.P.*, Naves, pp. 235–36. Quite likely it is Voltaire's dilettante approach to philosophy which keeps him from pursuing a very serious "analysis" of thinking, and just as likely his prejudice against medievals which prevented his studying seriously what previous ages had thought on the subject. See also *Remarques sur les Pensées de M. Pascal* (1728), Moland, XXII, 54.

[35] *Remarques sur les Pensées de M. Pascal*, Moland, XXII, 56. One must keep in mind, however, in reading the *Remarques,* that Voltaire's purpose was to discredit his opponent, and that, under other circumstances, Voltaire would not necessarily have made the same statements. For a consideration of the Voltaire-Pascal controversy on the body-soul question, see Mina

Furthermore, man's ideas are so lacking in clarity and certitude, so limited, that they are scarcely deserving of the high evaluation Pascal gives them. No one knows even how a piece of wood is turned into charcoal, how lime heats water, how an animal heart begins to beat, or what causes sensations, ideas, memories. Even the essence of matter is no more known to man than it is to children who touch its surfaces. The limits of the human mind are almost at the end of the human nose.[36] Not only is the mind limited in what it can know, but also in the degree of certitude it can have. Before the time of Copernicus, everyone would have agreed that the sun rose in the east and set in the west; they were *certain* of it. And yet they were wrong. It is only with demonstrations like those of geometry that one acquires certitude; other so-called demonstrations yield only probabilities. Yet, Voltaire says, his own existence, his thoughts, and his moods are all as certain to him as the propositions of geometry, for these occurrences are proved by the principle of noncontradiction. That is, the argument runs, he cannot exist and not exist, think and not think, feel sad and not feel sad.

Such reasoning is evidently more an effect of Voltaire's desire to justify his common sense than of any inclination to be strictly scientific, for a more magnificent example of begging the question could be found only with difficulty. What the argument really means is that *if* he exists he does not not-exist, etc.; and to prove the consequent, the antecedent is assumed to be true. Quite obviously, however, Voltaire did not consider his argument otherwise than flawless, for he asserts that the physical certitude he has of his existence and of his feelings is of the same value, though not the same kind, as mathematical certitude. But of certitudes founded on appearances or on the unanimous agreement of men, the same thing cannot be said.[37]

Waterman, *Voltaire, Pascal and Human Destiny* (Morningside Heights, New York: King's Crown Press, 1942), pp. 25–27.

[36] "Bornes de l'esprit humain" (1764), *D.P.*, Naves, p. 60. See also, "Qualités occultes" (1774), *Q.E.*, Moland, XX, 132: "Occult qualities have for a very long time been laughed at, but it would be better to ridicule those who do not believe in them. Every principle, every primary source of all the works which come from the hand of the demiurge, is occult and hidden forever from mere men. What is centripetal force? the force of gravitation which acts at such immense distances? . . . Everything around us, everything within us is an enigma which man cannot solve . . . the more I read, the more I can assert that I know nothing."

[37] "Certain, certitude" (1764), *D.P.*, Naves, pp. 99–100.

In his *Cambridge Notebook*, Voltaire lists many of the things about which he does not have a mathematical certitude or any other kind of certitude:

> I do not know what matter is, and still less what spirit is; whether there is a God or whether there is not; whether the world is finite or infinite, created or eternal, arranged by an intelligence or by physical laws, or even by chance. I will never understand how I think, how I retain my thoughts, how I move about. The first principles upon which my existence is dependent are unknowable. Therefore, it is not these principles that I ought to seek to know, but rather what is useful and dangerous to the human body, the laws by which the body moves, not why it moves. . . . [I ought to seek] to get a good yield from my land, not to understand how the wheat grows.[38]

That is, since the human reason is so limited, one might as well relinquish speculation and direct one's energies into more pragmatic channels. Voltaire, of course, was not always pessimistic concerning his ability to attain certitude, but there is throughout his works evidence of half-hearted efforts to understand, followed by a feeling of frustration and repeated protestations of his ignorance. Nevertheless, Voltaire also had his optimistic moments, when he erred in the opposite direction, as witness his "eight laws" stating the mathematical proportions between the mass and motion of fire as it spreads.[39] Moreover, after his brief

---

[38] "Je ne scaurois [sic] comprendre ce que c'est la matière, encore moins ce que c'est qu'esprit. S'il y a un dieu, s'il n'y en a point, si le monde est fini ou infini, créé ou éternel, arrangé par intelligence ou par loix physiques, encore moins par hazard. Je ne saurois comprendre comment je pense, comment je retiens mes pensées, comment je remue. Les premiers principes aux lequels mon existence est attachée sont tous impénétrables. Ce n'est donc pas cela qu'il faut chercher, mais ce qui est utile, et dangereux, au corps humain, les lois par les quels il se meut, non prquoy il se meut . . . tâcher de rendre une terre fertile, non rechercher comment le blé peut croître." Cambridge Notebook, *Voltaire's Notebooks*, edited by Theodore Besterman (2 vols., Genève: Institut et Musée Voltaire, 1952), I, 74. The *Notebooks* consist principally of previously unpublished Voltairian jottings. Besterman divides the jottings into five "notebooks": the small Leningrad notebook, dating from 1726 to about 1728, found among the books and papers sold to Empress Catherine II of Russia by Mme Denis, Voltaire's niece; the Cambridge notebook, dating from 1727 to about 1730; the major Leningrad group of notebooks, the *sottisier* gathered together by Wagnière, Voltaire's secretary, and dating from about 1735 to 1750; the Paris notebooks, from about 1740 to 1750, with two entries from 1766 to 1767; and, finally, the Piccini notebooks, mostly from 1750 to 1755, plus two paragraphs from 1778.

[39] *Essai sur la nature du feu* (1738), Moland, XXII, 309.

British period of skepticism concerning the ability to prove the existence of God, Voltaire gave every evidence of regarding his proofs as almost mathematically certain.

Here is manifested another of Voltaire's inconsistencies: while he is willing to grant that the existence of God can be proved from the evidence available to the senses, he will not grant the same of the immaterial soul, though his reasons for refusing to grant the existence of the soul would apply equally well to the existence of God. That is, he grants that God exists and is immaterial, but he cannot grant the existence of an immaterial soul, because it is impossible to have a sense image of something immaterial. Four thousand volumes of metaphysics, he says, will not suffice to teach one what the soul is.[40] Geometry has taught man many truths, but metaphysics has taught very few.[41] Because the objects of metaphysics are immaterial things, things which are *trans naturam*, and therefore are not capable of being represented by the imagination, they cannot be known in themselves. The existence of God can be known by his works, but beyond this, metaphysics is often a romance suitable to minds which would rather enjoy pleasant dreams than wear themselves out with the hard work of such sciences as geometry.[42] Moreover, it would be much simpler to admit that thinking matter is possible and there is, then, no need for positing an immaterial substance such as a soul.

Not only is the metaphysician's claim to the existence of a soul without foundation; the contention of some metaphysicians that this soul is immortal is nothing but an incentive to laughter. At least, Voltaire himself can only laugh when he is told that man will still have ideas when he no longer has senses. When a man has lost his nose, his nose is no more a part of him anymore than is the polar star. When death deprives him of *all* his parts so that he is no longer a man, it is difficult to maintain that there still remain the ideas which are the result of the parts that have been lost. It would be easier for Voltaire to admit that a man eats after death than to claim that he continues to think after the dissolution of his sense organs. If the latter claim could be validly made, then one might as easily say that a man's laughter survives his death, or that a bird's song continues to exist after the bird has ceased to

---

[40] "Ame" (1770), *Q.E.*, Naves, pp. 430–31.
[41] "Matière" (1764), *D.P.*, Naves, p. 298.
[42] "Métaphysique" (1771), *Q.E.*, Moland, XX, 76.

be. Of course, God *could* have given man an immortal soul, but before a philosopher could assert this he would have to see it.[43]

Furthermore, if one does not even know the nature of a soul, how can one be bold enough to assert that immortality is of its essence? Still further, if man did not exist yesterday, would a cautious thinker dare maintain that a part of him will exist eternally? Should one posit immortality in man just because immortality is something men desire? It would, of course, be most consoling if one could survive death, if the more excellent part of oneself were to be preserved eternally, if one could live forever with one's friends. Doubtless, Voltaire adds, it was to obtain such consolation that the peoples of the Orient invented the system of metempsychosis.[44]

Nevertheless, in a letter written to Jean Baptiste Nicholas Formont, in 1733, Voltaire points out that the theory that God has given to matter the faculty of thought is in conformity with Christianity, for immortality can be attached to matter, about which we know so little, as well as it can be attached to spirit, about which we know even less.[45] How little this conceded to Christianity, however, is evident from a jotting in the *Leningrad Notebook:* "Father Malebranche set forth the resurrection of insects in proof of the pretended resurrection of our souls. He was as mistaken on the first point as on the second." [46]

The contrast between the two foregoing points of view reflects, perhaps, Voltaire's internal battle over the question of immortality. With his notions of thought as a function of the body and of personal identity as a concatenation of memories, he was unable to understand how the person could survive the dissolution of the body. Nevertheless, the possibility that there was something immortal about man was never disproved to Voltaire's

---

[43] *Traité,* c. iv, "Si ce qu'on appelle âme est immortel," Moland, XXII, 213–14.

[44] *Ibid.,* p. 214. Voltaire seems to overlook here the fact that Oriental—and Greek—theories of metempsychosis have not always been of the consoling variety.

[45] Letter of c. August 15, 1733, *Correspondence,* Besterman, III, 127.

[46] *Voltaire's Notebooks,* I, 219: "Le père Malebranche, aportoit les résurrections des insectes, en preuve de la résurrection prétendue de nos âmes. Il se trompoit sur le premier fait, aussi bien que sur le second." On the same page in the Besterman edition, there is a rather interesting reflection which might have given pause to Voltaire: "Skepticism destroys all and destroys itself at the same time, as Samson was crushed under the ruins of the temple."

complete satisfaction. It is a fact of psychological interest that Voltaire did not treat this question quite so cavalierly as some other, perhaps more academic, questions. Quite often he argues that something or other *cannot* be the case because he is unable to understand how it could be the case. On the question of human immortality, however, he generally concedes at least some slight possibility of an affirmative answer, even though he is unable to imagine how such a possibility could be realized.

In *The Princess of Babylon*, for instance, the phoenix is made to say that it is no more difficult for God to grant again, after a lapse of time, the sensation, memory, and thought that the phoenix had possessed before death than to continue granting those functions throughout the bird's life. The phoenix expresses itself as ignorant of *how* this regeneration is brought about, whether God has granted the functions of life to a single fiery atom or to the organic composite, but this is just one more instance of the ignorance of creatures.[47]

Something similar occurs in the *Lettres de Memmius à Cicéron:*

> I can neither deny nor affirm that the great being wills to continue granting us after our death the same gifts we now enjoy, that he could attach the faculty of thinking to some part of ourselves which would subsist after death; I have proof neither for nor against such a state of affairs. It is up to the person who asserts such a strange thing to prove it clearly; and inasmuch as no one until now has done so, one may be permitted to doubt.[48]

This rather reluctant admission of a possibility is immediately followed, however, by several arguments against immortality.

> When we are only dust, of what value will it be to us that an atom of this dust passes into some creature endowed with the same faculties that this atom enjoyed during life? This new person will no more be I than I will be this cabbage or this melon formed from the earth in which I shall have been buried. In order that I should be

---

[47] *La Princesse de Babylone* (1768), Moland, XXI, 292–93.

[48] *Lettres de Memmius à Cicéron*, Moland, XXVIII, 459–60. "Que le grand Etre veuille persévérer à nous continuer les mêmes dons après notre mort; qu'il puisse attacher la faculté de penser à quelque partie de nous-mêmes qui subsistera encore, à la bonne heure: je ne veux ni l'affirmer ni le nier; je n'ai de preuve ni pour ni contre. Mais c'est à celui qui affirme une chose si étrange à la prouver clairement; et comme jusqu'ici personne ne l'a fait, on me permettra de douter."

truly immortal, I would have to conserve my organs, my memory, all my faculties. Open all the tombs, reassemble all the bones; you will never find anything there which will give you the least glimmering of this hope.[49]

Perhaps Voltaire's occasional, rather embarrassed, somewhat secretive, half-sincere gestures of returning to the practice of his childhood faith were not entirely motivated by concern for his safety in this life, but also by some haunting fear that there might be, after all, another life in which justice would be meted out.

Such, then, is Voltaire's analysis of human nature and its capabilities: man differs from other animals merely by being able to receive a greater variety of ideas; his ideas are given to him by God, just as matter receives its motion from God. The ideas which man receives are all fundamentally ideas of sensible realities, though man can, by use of his imagination, form "abstract" ideas; man has no soul; he is organized matter to which God gives life, sensations, and ideas. Consequently, there is no reason for holding that man will continue to live or think once his body has been dissolved by death. It remains to be seen whether man can be said to be a free agent or whether he is as completely determined by God as is the inanimate world, and whether, in consequence, Voltaire assigns to man any relation to God different from that of inanimate beings.

---

[49] *Ibid.*, p. 60. "Quand nous ne sommes plus que cendre, de quoi nous servirait-il qu'un atome de cette cendre passât dans quelque créature, revêtu des mêmes facultés dont il aurait joui pendant sa vie? Cette personne nouvelle ne sera pas plus ma personne, cet étranger ne sera pas plus moi que je ne serait ce chou ou ce melon qui se seront formés de la terre où j'aurait été inhumé. Pour que je fusse véritablement immortel, il faudrait que je conservasse mes organes, ma mémoire, toutes mes facultés. Ouvrez tous les tombeaux, rassemblez tous les ossements, vous ne trouverez rien qui vous donne la moindre lueur de cette espérance."

CHAPTER FOUR

Human Freedom

IF THERE IS TO BE, in Voltaire's conception of the universe, any activity differing from that of inanimate objects, all of whose activities are determined by a geometrizing God acting according to immutable laws, such activity would be most apt to be found in men exercising some degree of autonomy through "free choice." It is for this reason that the question of human freedom is so crucial for an understanding of Voltaire's constructive deism. And, perhaps, it is the urgency of the question which accounts for Voltaire's twice changing his mind on the subject. The reasons for these changes of opinion give some added insight into Voltaire's over-all theory of the relation of the universe to God. We shall, then, take up in this chapter the *philosophe's* doctrine of free will as expressed in several of his more important philosophical works: the *Treatise on Metaphysics*, the *Elements of Newton's Philosophy*, and the *Philosophical Dictionary*.

The question of human freedom, Voltaire says in the *Treatise in Metaphysics*, is really a very simple one, despite the efforts of some philosophers to enshroud it in mystery. Freedom is simply the power of acting. *La liberté est uniquement le pouvoir d'agir.*[1] If a stone were capable of moving itself by its own choice it would be free. Men and animals have this ability; therefore, they are free. A man is conscious of having within himself the power of acting, of moving his body, of applying his thought to what he wills. If this consciousness were only an illusion, then God, who is the cause of such a conviction that man has a will, would be acting in a manner absurd in an infinitely wise being. Nor can one object that it is unworthy of a philosopher to have recourse to God in giving a reasonable argument. Voltaire shows, in the *Treatise*, after offering his arguments for the existence of God, that, if man is free, God is the cause of that freedom. But if man

---

[1] *Traité*, Moland, XXII, 216.

is not free, God is the cause of man's error in thinking himself free. Nor could it be matter, which of itself has no intelligence, that would account for the inner conviction of freedom in man.

Man really has a will; therefore, he is really an agent. To will and to act are precisely the same thing as to be free. God himself could not be free in any other sense. He has willed and he has acted according to his will. If one were to assert that God was determined necessarily in his willing, one would be asserting something every bit as ridiculous as one who asserts both that there is a God and there is no God. If God were necessitated he would no longer be an agent; he would be a patient, and so would not be God.[2] Freedom in God is the power to think always what he wishes, and to effect always what he wishes. The freedom given by God to man, however, is a feeble power limited to enabling men to entertain some thoughts and to effect certain movements.[3] Children and brute animals have the freedom to will and to effect movements of their bodies, but they have no freedom to think as they wish.[4]

The fact that men are sometimes driven by violent passion to actions they do not will (as is the case when a man who prefers a peaceful life is impelled by ambition to enter into competition with others) is not sufficient to prove that man is not truly free. Analogously, the fact that men are sometimes ill is not sufficient to prove that they are never well. On the contrary, illness would have no meaning except in relation to health, and man's consciousness of being compelled occasionally by his passions is incomprehensible except in relation to the freedom of which such compulsion is a limitation. Not to be able to control one's passions by the will is similar to a paralysis of the limbs; one is simply not able to effect what he wills. However, if one were to be completely dominated by violent passion all his life or be so obsessed that he could never have the ideas he wished to have, then it could only be said that he lacked that part of man which consists in the ability of sometimes thinking what one wishes to think.[5]

Just as men differ in the degree to which they possess other de-

---

[2] *Ibid.*, p. 217.

[3] *Ibid.*, pp. 217–18.

[4] When Voltaire attempts to explain in later years what he means by freedom, it becomes clear that only God is free in any of the usual senses of "free," and that even then he is free only from coercion by another.

[5] *Traité*, Moland, XXII, 218.

sirable human qualities, so they differ in their degree of freedom; freedom is the health of the soul, and very few persons are completely and unalterably healthy. By attempting to acquire the habit of reflection, one can strengthen his will, but it is useless to expect ever to have a complete control of all one's desires; there will always be some involuntary movements in the soul, just as there are in the body.[6] If one were to be free always, he would be as God. The fact, however, that man has not the freedom of God is no reason why man should deny the limited degree of liberty that he does have.[7]

In addition to those who deny man's liberty because he is sometimes overwhelmed by passion, there are others who deny the same fact, but do so on the ground that man's understanding is not capable of judging otherwise than it does, and his will is determined by his judgment. It is certainly true, Voltaire admits, that man cannot will anything unless the idea of that thing is present to him; for example, he would certainly never will to attend the theatre unless the idea of the theatre were present to him and present as something agreeable. However, it is precisely in this that his liberty consists: he has the power of determining himself to do that which does appear agreeable to him. To will what would not be pleasurable is a formal contradiction and an impossibility.[8] It cannot be questioned that man determines himself to what seems to him the best, but the fact that he *has* within himself the motive force to determine himself is the crucial point; to be able to do what pleases one is to be free.[9] The reason why the

---

[6] *Ibid.*, p. 219. "Il y aura toujours dans notre âme comme dans notre corps des mouvements involontaires." Voltaire's distinction between movements of the body and movements of the soul, his comparison of the health of the body with freedom, the health of the soul (*la liberté est la santé de l'âme*), would seem to indicate a habit of thought which was not completely alien to the Cartesian doctrine of body and soul, despite Voltaire's protests that he knows nothing of what the soul might be, other than that which men and brutes have in common.

[7] *Ibid.* In the *Discours en vers sur l'homme*, "De la liberté" (1734), Moland, IX, 388–92, Voltaire again compares human freedom with divine liberty. Man resembles God, who conceives, wishes, and acts. Man conceives, wills, acts, and so is free.

[8] *Traité*, Moland, XXII, 219. "Or, c'est en cela même que consiste sa liberté: c'est le pouvoir de se déterminer soi-même à faire ce qui lui paraît bon; vouloir ce que ne lui ferait pas plaisir est une contradiction formelle et une impossibilité."

[9] *Ibid.*, p. 220. Unfortunately, Voltaire does not make clear what he means

enemies of freedom make such an egregious error is that they have reified "will" and "understanding," whereas, in fact, these are only abstract ideas invented to facilitate discourse. They mean, in reality, no more than "man willing" and "man thinking." There is, then, no possibility of man's understanding acting upon his will. Man understands and man wills. Depending upon the degree of liberty he enjoys, he may be able to have the ideas that he wishes to have; then, if any of these ideas should present a thing as desirable, he can move his physical powers to actions ordered toward attaining that thing.[10]

To one familiar with the medieval subtleties in writings dealing with free will, Voltaire's explanation is apt to be somewhat unsatisfactory. The *philosophe* gives no evidence of having seen that the problem of human freedom involves at least two crucial questions: in what sense, if any, is it true to say that man has any part in determining what shall appear to him as desirable or preferable; and, if a thing does appear as desirable or preferable, is that all that is involved in his choosing it? That is, at just what point in considering, judging, and acting to obtain the desired goal does freedom enter in? Is it prior to the judgment of desirability? Is it in some internal but nonphysical consent to the judgment? Is it simply in the ability of applying the physical powers to the attainment of what is desired; or are all these activities within the ambit of man's free choice? It would seem that Voltaire has reduced the whole problem almost to the simplicity of saying that man is free because he can do what he wants. Such an assertion does not explain the determination of the wanting, which is one of the points at issue.

---

by "determine himself"; in the context of the previous argument; however, to determine oneself seems to be only to move one's mental, emotional, or physical powers to act. W. H. Barber, in his *Leibniz in France, from Arnauld to Voltaire*, pp. 199–200, notes a similarity between Voltaire's thought here and that of Leibniz: "These views of Voltaire's, which implicitly exclude the possibility of a liberty of indifference, are clearly in harmony with those expressed by Leibniz in the *Théodicée* and the correspondence with Clarke. Both insist that the existence of motives for action does not destroy true liberty, although Voltaire, following Locke, sees the essence of liberty in the absence of physical restraints upon the exercise of the will, whereas for Leibniz the further condition must be fulfilled that choice is not directed by any logical necessity, that the individual is faced with alternatives which are themselves contingent."

[10] *Traité*, Moland, XXII, 220.

Lightly though Voltaire may consider the nature of human freedom, he is most earnest in offering several additional arguments for its reality. If man is not free, he says, then it must be the case that God is eternally occupied with acting for man, determining him, and tricking him into believing that he is free. In this case at least God would be free, and freedom possible. If freedom is possible, there is no reason for denying it to man.[11]

Yet, even granted that God would be the cause of man's determination if man were not free, this would be, according to Voltaire's general outlook on the matter, only by means of natural laws which stem from God's nature as a geometrizing creator. In Voltaire's opinion, freedom for God is simply the complete absence of coercion from without; but Voltaire would not for one moment grant that man is free from all external coercion. Moreover, Voltaire has, on more than one occasion, noted that human attributes are not at all like the divine attributes designated by the same names; thus, "freedom" as predicated of God would have no meaning when predicated of man.[12]

To those who object that man is determined by pleasure, Voltaire retorts that they have themselves admitted man's freedom without being aware of having done so, for to do what pleases one is to be free. God is free in this very manner; that is, he can act only according to his pleasure (*Il ne peut opérer que selon son plaisir*). Consequently, if one denies freedom to man because man is determined by what pleases him, then one must also deny it to God, who is also determined by his pleasure.[13]

There is, in the *Treatise on Metaphysics*, still one more argument to be considered: God knows with absolute certitude what will occur in the future; therefore, what he foresees will eventuate without fail. Consequently, man is not free to do otherwise than God has from all eternity foreseen that he will do. What does this reasoning prove, asks Voltaire? Nothing other than that we do not know, and cannot know, anything at all of the divine prescience, that all the divine attributes are for us impenetrable mysteries.[14] The perennial dispute about God's prescience has caused

---

[11] *Ibid.*
[12] See *Il faut prendre un parti* (1772), Moland, XXVIII, 534.
[13] *Traité*, Moland, XXII, 220.
[14] *Ibid.*

nothing but dissension, and it would cost very little for the dissenters simply to admit that they do not know what they are talking about and to cease making of a sacred science a miserable charlatanism.[15] It would not appear to be unreasonably harsh if one were to suspect Voltaire of being considerably less concerned with the dignity of theology than with disposing of a very inconvenient difficulty by recourse to an *argumentum ad hominem.* The problem is a genuine one, and, while the solutions traditionally offered have not been such as to lay the ghost of the problem permanently, at least to have seen the difficulty and to have considered it seriously is an accomplishment surpassing Voltaire's scornful aspersions. Nonetheless, the scholastics who struggled with the question would have agreed completely with Voltaire that its perfect solution would demand an impossible comprehension of the divine essence.[16]

In that part of the *Elements of Newton's Philosophy* which Voltaire composed about 1740 and which was first published separately as *Newton's Metaphysics*, there is a section on human freedom. According to Newton and Clarke, Voltaire tells us, the infinitely free being has communicated to man a limited portion of his own freedom, not merely the simple ability of applying his thought to such and such an object and of inaugurating certain motions, but the very faculty of willing with a complete and efficacious will, without any reason other than this willing itself. Nor is there anyone on earth who is not at least sometimes conscious that he possesses such freedom. On closer investigation, the freedom which man possesses turns out to be of two kinds, a freedom of spontaneity and a freedom of indifference.[17] When one has motives, which are always the effect of the understanding or

---

[15] *Ibid.*, pp. 220–21.

[16] Ira Wade, in his *Studies on Voltaire*, pp. 89–90, writes that Voltaire is confused about what he is trying to do in Chapter VII of the *Traité* and that, as a consequence, the structure and the ideas of the chapter are confused. Wade is of the opinion, however, that these defects are not found in the *extrait d'un chapitre sur la liberté* which Voltaire sent to Crown Prince Frederick. Wade calls the *extrait* "a neatly and carefully arranged work in distinct contrast to the carelessly organized Chapter VII." This may well be true, but neat and careful arrangement have little bearing on the philosophical content of the *extrait*, which is in almost perfect accord with Chapter VII of the *Traité*. The *extrait* is printed in Wade's *Studies on Voltaire*, pp. 92–108.

[17] *Eléments*, Moland, XXII, 414. This distinction is something not at all

of instinct, one's will determines itself by them. Thus, if one's understanding represents to itself that it is better to obey the law than to violate it, one obeys the law with a freedom of spontaneity; one does voluntarily what the last dictate of one's understanding obliges him to do.

Spontaneous freedom is most evident when there is question of combating one's passions. Though the passion may be violent, one's understanding may conclude that the passion ought to be resisted, and so the understanding represents withstanding the passion as a greater good than succumbing to it. This last motive is the impelling one; one does, by reason of it, not what one's passion would desire, but what one wills. In such a case one has all the freedom such circumstances could possibly admit.[18]

The circumstances are different when there is question of liberty of indifference. Here there is no pleasure or distaste involved. For example, if someone is requested to turn to the right or to the left when neither alternative is productive of more or less pleasure or distaste than the other, he chooses, not because of any motive outside his will, but simply and solely because he wills.[19] Nor is it reasonable to object that one who chooses merely because he so desires to choose, acts as one demented. The idiot and the mentally deranged are persons who are ill and have no freedom at all; whatever they do is determined for them by the pathological state of their physical organs. They are not masters of themselves; they choose nothing. It is only the man who is able to determine himself who is free.[20]

Moreover, it is a mistake to think that there is no motive in a choice proceeding from the liberty of indifference, that the

---

found in the *Traité*, nor is there indicated in the former work any meaning of freedom in man other than the ability to direct one's thought and inaugurate certain physical motions. However, Voltaire does not explain in the *Eléments* just what he *means* by the faculty of willing with a complete and efficacious will, though the context of the definition gives some reason for thinking that this is merely a definition of the liberty of indifference as distinct from the freedom of spontaneity.

[18] *Ibid*. In this passage, however, there is nothing to indicate whether succumbing to one's passions would be a matter of free choice as well.

[19] *Ibid.*, p. 413.

[20] *Ibid.*, p. 414. If Voltaire were to be classified among those who have worked seriously at the problem of explaining human freedom, it would be necessary, on the basis of this theory of liberty of indifference, to classify him as a voluntarist—but only where there is question of indifferent objects, and even in this case, the true determining factor is an idea. Where there is

choice is without cause. The motive lies in the fact that one possibility or the other presents itself to the mind at the moment of making the choice. Just as everything else has its cause, so does such a choice; the cause is the last idea that one has received before choosing. Although Voltaire seemed not to be aware of it, this makes even the liberty of indifference a question of "intellectual" determinism; if one cannot determine what the last idea shall be, then he is as much a pawn of fate as any material body governed by immutable natural laws.[21]

Apparently Voltaire was no more satisfied than anyone else that he had cleared up all the difficulties which hedge around the problem of human freedom, for in the 1756 edition of the *Eléments* he adds a new chapter on "Doutes sur la liberté qu'on nomme d'indifférence," a chapter which consists almost entirely of questions, with only one or two suggestions for their answers: Could it be that ideas are absolutely different just because they are entertained in different brains? That is, could ideas, just because they are in a human rather than an animal brain, be productive of freedom? Are men not determined by their instincts just as much as brute animals are? Is instinct not what is meant by a man's temperament? Is an act of choice not always the effect of the last idea that one has received? Since these ideas are necessary and not free, is not the act of choice also necessitated? Was Locke not correct in calling freedom "power"? Are not men automata born to will always, to do sometimes what they will and sometimes the contrary? Whatever man thinks of these questions, Voltaire concludes, the wheels which move the machinery of the universe will continue to turn just the same.[22]

It appears, then, that Voltaire has returned, after an excursus

---

question of a difference in the pleasure value of the possible objects, Voltaire's theory seems to be that of intellectual determinism; the will follows blindly the intellect's necessitated judgment.

[21] *Ibid.*, p. 415. In the edition of 1751, Voltaire adds that what this last idea depends upon is the condition of one's physical organs. This would seem to make "freedom" compatible with what appears to be a species of "physical determinism."

[22] *Ibid.*, pp. 417–18. If Wade is correct in his opinion that Voltaire was reworking the section on free will in the *Treatise on Metaphysics* as late as 1738, and corresponding with Frederick on the question of freedom at this very time, it is quite possible that the defense of freedom of indifference in the *Eléments* represents some part of the discussion with Frederick and that the added chapter, "Doutes sur la liberté qu'on nomme d'indifférence," was

into the realms of liberty, to his pristine, Lockean viewpoint that freedom, if it means anything at all, means only the ability to do what one has necessarily decided to do. In fact, Voltaire's entire psychology, if one excepts the attempted defense of freedom of indifference in the *Treatise on Metaphysics,* is not much more than a reiteration of his exposition of the Lockean psychology in the early *Philosophical Letters.*[23]

---

one of the fruits of the discussion, as well as of reading Anthony Collins' *Philosophical Inquiry Concerning Human Liberty* (London: 1717). In 1738, in the letter with which he enclosed two chapters of "a work on ethics," Voltaire writes to Frederick that God could not be the cause of all man's choices, for then God would be guilty of deceiving man by making him think he was free; that God could well give man a share of his own freedom and that such a communication would not impede God's infinite power, for the shared freedom would itself be an effect of that power; that the divine foreknowledge cannot be an objection to true freedom, for God does not actually know the future. In fact, Voltaire suggests that God will find entertainment and escape from ennui in being surprised by what his creatures will do. Finally, Voltaire asks Frederick to consider the consequences for human life, friendship, honor, and heroism if one denies that man is free. Letter of January 23, 1738, *Correspondence,* Besterman, VII, 37. The freedom which Voltaire is championing here is not the mere ability to *do* what one pleases; it is at least the ability to overcome one's desires by an act of willing; it is in some sense a freedom which escapes complete determination in the very act of choice. In a letter dated several months after that just cited, Voltaire writes to Frederick: "The more I look into myself the more I believe myself to be free. . . . It is a feeling that all other men have just as I do. It is the invariable principle of our conduct. The most radical partisans of absolute fatalism all direct their own conduct according to principles of freedom. . . . Why did the Author of their nature give them this feeling of freedom if they do not actually have such a freedom? Why such deceit in a being who is truth itself? . . . All our other feelings are true; God does not deceive us in the desire that we have to be happy, to drink, to eat, to multiply our species. When we feel certain desires, these desires certainly exist . . . when we have thoughts it is very clear that we are thinking. What then? Shall the feeling of liberty be the only one by which the infinitely perfect being will amuse himself by creating an absurd illusion? . . . There is no middle ground; either we are automata which do nothing and in which God does all, or we are agents, that is, free creatures. But I ask what proof there is that we are simple automata and that this interior feeling of freedom is an illusion?" In the same letter Voltaire goes on to state that all the arguments against freedom can be reduced to the objection that what God foreknows will happen will necessarily happen; this objection does not hold good for one who denies, as does Voltaire, that there is such a thing as prescience in God. Letter of March 8, 1738, *Correspondence,* Besterman, VII, 105–07. Nevertheless, in the end Voltaire abandoned his theory of freedom of indifference and became a champion of the absolute fatality advocated by Frederick.

[23] See *Lettres philosophiques* (1734), Lettre XIII, "Sur Locke," edited by Raymond Naves (Paris: Garnier, 1939), pp. 66–68.

It would seem that this return to an original position was the ultimate result of a more vigorous application of Voltaire's metaphysical principle that nothing occurs without a cause, a principle very much like Leibniz' principle of sufficient reason. Freedom of indifference, seeming to Voltaire to be an instance of uncaused activity, came to be unthinkable, a violation of a self-evident principle. Having finally settled upon the conclusion that freedom can be nothing other than the ability to do what one wishes, regardless of how one's wishes are determined, Voltaire professes to be unable to understand how "free will" can be understood in any other way.

In *The Ignorant Philosopher*, written about twenty-five years after the *Elements*, Voltaire gives us his own version of how he came to adopt a deterministic attitude on the question of man's freedom. He read, he says, the medieval philosophers, such as Thomas Aquinas, and was as much in the dark as they were. Then he read Locke and found some light shed on the subject, light which was augmented by Collins' treastise on human freedom. After having studied these two great men, Voltaire was never able to find anything which could give him more instruction on the subject. What he gathered from their writings was, in summary: everything has its cause; an effect without a cause is unintelligible. Every act of willing is the consequence of a judgment which is, in turn, necessary. Freedom consists in doing what one wills, in having power; the choice itself is necessary, because it is caused by the last idea that one has before the choice is made. It would be strange, indeed, if all nature, all the planets should obey necessary laws, while man, a little and insignificant animal, should be able to act as he pleased, from sheer caprice.[24]

---

[24] *Le Philosophe ignorant* (1766) Moland, XXVI, 55–57. Voltaire adds here that he cannot forgive Dr. Clarke for having opposed these truths, which were evident to him but did not fit into his system. It is quite probable that Dr. Clarke had as much to do as anyone with Voltaire's earlier acceptance of indifference in man's choices, for it was at the time of writing the *Eléments*, therefore at a time when he was giving special attention to Newton and Clarke, that Voltaire wrote his defense of freedom in the nondeterministic sense of the term.

Norman Torrey, in *Voltaire and the English Deists*, pp. 57–58, gives his interpretation of Voltaire's intellectual journey on the question of human freedom.

Collins' influence can readily be seen in several passages from the *Philosophical Inquiry Concerning Human Liberty*, p. 11: "Man is a *necessary Agent*, if all his actions are so determined by the causes preceding each action, that not one past action could possibly not have come to pass, or have

In the *Philosophical Dictionary* there is printed a dialogue on the crucial problem of man's freedom of choice. It is the Lockean explanation which is defended. A man at whom a battery of cannon is shooting cannot help but will to run to shelter; to will otherwise he would have to be insane. The case is similar to that of a dog which sees a rabbit. The freedom of both man and dog consists in being able to do what they wish: the man can run for shelter; the dog can chase the rabbit. Nor ought one to bemoan the fact that human freedom is not of a different kind from the freedom possible to brutes. There is a sufficient difference of degree, for a man is capable of having many more and much more complex ideas than a brute animal. Consequently, man is able to do more things than a brute animal and is, therefore, more free. Freedom is, after all, only the power of doing what one wishes. To say that one is free to marry, for example, is only to say that one is free to sign a marriage contract.

Nor can one justly claim such a thing as liberty of indifference, for to say that one wills just because one wills, is to posit an effect without a cause. Furthermore, if one says that the reason for the choice is that the idea of the thing chosen was the last idea in the mind before the choice was made, then one is only denying that the choice is free and is admitting that the action was determined.[25] It is not one's will that is free, but one's actions, provided

---

been otherwise than it was; nor one future action can possibly not come to pass, or be otherwise than it shall be. He is a *free Agent*, if he is able, at any time under the circumstances and causes he then is, to do different things: Or, in other words, If he is not ever unavoidably determin'd in every point of time by the circumstances he is in, and causes he is under, to do that one thing he does, and not possibly to do any other." Pp. 57–59: "If any thing can have a beginning which has no cause, then nothing can produce something. And if nothing can produce something, then the world might have had a beginning without a cause; which is not only an absurdity commonly charged on Atheists, but is a real absurdity in it self. Besides, if a cause be not a necessary cause, it is no cause at all. For if causes are not necessary causes, then causes are not suited to or are indifferent to effects . . . . a cause suited to the effect is a necessary cause; for if it does not produce the effect, it is not suited to it, or is no cause at all of it. Liberty, therefore, or a power to act or not to act, to do this or another thing under the same causes, is an *Impossibility* and *Atheistical*."

[25] "Liberté" (1764), *D.P.*, Naves, pp. 274–77. Interestingly enough, this is one of the very objections to liberty of indifference that Voltaire attempts to answer in defending such a freedom in the *Eléments*. Moreover, what is regarded in the *Dictionnaire* as a reason for rejecting liberty of indifference is taken as supplying the required cause in the *Eléments*: namely, that the last idea one has before choosing is the necessitating cause of the effect.

that one is not impeded from accomplishing what one has necessarily willed. An addition dated 1771 adduces a further objection against a theory of liberty of indifference. If there is freedom only when there is question of indifferent objects, such as walking up and down four times rather than five, or of sleeping on the left or the right side, then the gift of such a freedom is just a joke.[26]

In sum, the only freedom which man has he has always, not only in matters which are of no importance. This freedom, however, is simply and solely the ability to do what he wishes. The man who is not completely able to have the thoughts he wishes or to perform the physical motions he desires is to that extent not free.

In the *Dictionary* article, "Free Choice," the problem is considered anew. Here it is stated flatly that Locke was quite correct in cutting the Gordian knot tied by philosophers and theologians disputing endlessly about whether or not man is free. It was Locke's contribution to have declared that liberty cannot belong to the will any more than color and motion. Freedom means simply "power" or it has no meaning at all. To say that the will *can* is as absurd as to say that the will is yellow or square. "Will," Voltaire says in a statement that can scarcely be doubted, "pertains to willing." What is not equally so clear is what he takes to be a corollary: *La volonté est le vouloir, et la liberté est le pouvoir.*[27] Freedom, then, does not belong to the will. There can be no willing without a cause, and the cause is nothing other than an agreeable idea, the predominant or determining idea, an idea which is *received*. To suppose uncaused choices would be to suppose a universe in which blind caprice plays a part. The intelligent man,

---

[26] This, again, is a complete reversal of the position Voltaire stated in the *Eléments*. It is quite possible, of course, that he was not sincere in his statements in the early editions of the *Eléments* before the addition of the chapter, "Doutes sur la liberté qu'on nomme d'indifférence," but was only being sufficiently cautious for the sake of a better and freer circulation of his work. This explanation, however, is not beyond criticism, both because of the correspondence being carried on with Frederick, in which Voltaire attempted to defend the freedom of indifference, and also because of other statements in the First Part of the *Eléments* which would have caused the work to be regarded unfavorably by the censors; e.g., the attacks on the soul as an entity different from the body, and the objections against immortality.

[27] "Franc arbitre," *D.P.*, Moland, XIX, 196–97: "Le mot de liberté n'appartient donc en aucune manière à la volonté." (Beuchot estimates that this article was written between 1765 and 1770. See Moland, XVII, viii–ix.)

however, realizes that there are just two possibilities: either the
world is one in which everything is an effect of the eternal design
of an absolute ruler, or it is one in which everything operates absolutely according to its nature. And in either case men are only
wheels in the world machinery.[28]

In an article written at approximately the same time as "Free
Choice," Voltaire has something more to say on the matter of
freedom, and makes some observations on the origin of man's
ideas. There is not, he tells us, from the lowest animal to the greatest philosopher, any being which can *will* motion, digestion, desire, love, instinct, or thought. That man actually does move, digest his food, have desires, love, experience instinctive drives,
think—all these actions are explicable if one realizes that God can,
without difficulty, work all these things in man without man's
knowing how they are done. There is no man who, if he looks
within himself, will not see that he is a mere puppet of Providence. Man thinks, but he does not give himself his thoughts.[29]
It is the God who formed him that gives thoughts to man. The fact
that thoughts occur in dreams is evidence that man does not cause
them himself. All human sentiency is involuntary; man has sense
experiences in spite of himself. He does nothing of himself; he is
nothing without the supreme power which does all things.[30]

Man, then, has a relationship to God quite similar to that of
inanimate beings. The difference lies principally in the fact that
God exercises his causality on nonliving things by moving them
immediately, whereas God moves men to action through the mediation of ideas. The degree of determination exercised by God,
however, is exactly the same for men and inanimate things. Because of the mediation of ideas, nonetheless, there arises in the
case of man the question of morality, the question of acting in
conformity with general moral principles. Inasmuch as the Vol-

---

[28] *Ibid.*, p. 198. It seems that the dichotomy of possibilities is not exhaus-
tive; at least, Voltaire has not demonstrated that there is no possible middle
ground. Nor is it quite in keeping with his periodic confessions of ignorance
that he should be certain that there are no possibilities of a universe different from the two he mentions.

[29] "Âme" (1770), *Q.E.*, Moland, XVII, 139. The interesting proof Voltaire adduces to show that man cannot give himself any thoughts is that, if
he gave himself his thoughts, he would know in advance which thoughts he
was going to have next. That this is impossible is evident: one can scarcely
think what he is going to think before he thinks it.

[30] *Ibid.* See also "Passions" (1774), *Q.E.*, Moland, XX, 179.

tairian theory of morality hinges upon the divine will and is, in effect, synonymous with "natural religion," it is another crucial point in the development of Voltaire's constructive deism. It remains to be seen, then, how Voltaire was able to develop a theory of morality founded on his psychological determinism.

CHAPTER FIVE

Morality

BECAUSE MAN, by his nature, is impelled to live in common with others of his kind, he is to some extent determined in his activities by his social situation. The relationship that man has to God cannot be understood, therefore, unless we understand man, one term of the relation, as he actually *is:* a member of society. As a consequence of man's natural inclination to live in society, human activities become more complex than the actions of brute animals and present, accordingly, a number of problems not encountered when there is question of brute animals. Among these problems, whose solution will help clarify the nature of man's relationship to God, Voltaire has given special attention to the following: the nature and origin of morality, the universality of certain moral laws, the existence of natural sanctions for moral law, the relationship between moral law and religion, man's knowledge of moral law, and the influence that belief in God has on the morality of those who are not *philosophes*. We shall, accordingly, treat of each of these problems as Voltaire has attempted to solve them.

The *Treatise on Metaphysics* contains a chapter entitled, "Man Considered as a Social Being," in which it is said that the author of nature has given to all animals not only an unconquerable instinct for whatever tends toward their individual conservation and the conservation of the species, but also a very powerful instinct for association with other members of the species. Man does not have the same sort of instinct for civil society as the ants and bees, but in virtue of man's needs, passions, and reason, he cannot long remain in a state of savagery. The love of man for woman and the love of both for their children impel them to industry and a crude beginning of the arts. Two families so formed find that they need each other, and new achievements eventuate from the new arrangement.

Further, man has not only the self-love (*l'amour-propre*) necessary for his own conservation, as have the other animals; he has also a natural benevolence (*bienveillance*) toward his own kind which disposes him toward union and cooperation with others. Such a feeling of benevolence, however, would never have sufficed for the foundation of great empires and flourishing cities, if man did not also have intense passions. Pride (*l'orgueil*) has been the principal instrument in the building of the civil order found on earth. Certain men were able to see that sacrificing a degree of their own well-being in making themselves useful to society would bring to them an ample reward in public esteem. There are, Voltaire says, two types of men: those godly men who sacrifice their self-love (*amour-propre*) to the public good, and those miserable men who love only themselves. Everyone would like to belong to the first class, but just as many are at heart members of the second. The desire to command drives men to be industrious, in order that they may convince others it would be advantageous to have them rule. Avarice adds daily to the progress of the arts. It is the passions alone which have united man and given rise to all the arts and delights of society. These passions are the works by means of which the Eternal Mechanic has animated and embellished nature; they are the wheels which keep the machinery running.[1]

Self-love (*amour-propre*) and all its ramifications are as necessary to man as the blood which flows in his veins; those who would like to take away man's passions because they are dangerous are like those who would like to drain a man of his blood because of the danger of a cerebral hemorrhage. The fact that many men have misused their passions is no reason for denying that the passions are useful.[2]

Society, which is an effect of man's self-love and his natural in-

---

[1] *Traité*, Moland, XXII, 221–24. See also Bernard de Mandeville, *An Enquiry into the Origin of Moral Virtue* (printed with *The Fable of the Bees*, 2 vols., Oxford: Clarendon Press, 1924), I, 41–45. Ira O. Wade, in his *Studies on Voltaire*, p. 47, points out how Mandeville's *Fable of the Bees* was an influence on Voltaire's ethical thought: "Both men regard vice and virtue as a social matter, both stress its relative character, both reject the idea of a religious, absolute, God-given code of conduct. Finally, both affirm its political origin, and stress how the passions, particularly pride and envy, were utilized to secure its origin." It seems quite probable, however, that Mandeville's influence was strongest during the time the *Traité de Métaphysique* was being written; some years later Voltaire appeared to be less inclined toward a wholly relativistic ethics than he was in the years at Cirey.

[2] *Traité*, Moland, XXII, 224.

stinct to associate himself with others of his kind, must have laws. Many of these necessary laws are determined by the interests, passions, and opinions of the law-makers or by the climate of the territory in which the society is established. For example, in some places it is considered a crime to drink wine, while in others intoxication is regarded as praiseworthy. Some nations demand that a man have no more than one wife, while others permit him as many as he can support; in Sparta adultery was encouraged, while the Athenians punished the adulterer with death. In many nations the title of king is regarded as sacred, while it is abominated in others. However, no matter what is enjoined or forbidden by the laws of a country, it is regarded as virtuous to observe the laws and as criminal to violate them. Though it does not make too much difference just what the rules are in a game of dice or cards, no one could play if some rules were not observed. Similarly, in a state it is not too important that the laws should forbid or enjoin this or that; the important matter is that they should be obeyed.[3]

Virtue and vice, in fact, are nothing other than what is useful and what is harmful to society. It has always been recognized in all countries that the most virtuous man is the one who most completely sacrifices his personal good for the public welfare; virtue is simply the habit of doing what pleases others, while vice is the habit of doing what displeases others. Thus, what is considered virtuous varies as greatly from one clime to another as do languages and dress.[4]

Despite the great variations in what is considered virtuous in various lands, it seems to Voltaire that there are some natural laws on which all men on earth must agree. Not that God has ever said to men, "Here are the laws which I give you from my own

---

[3] *Ibid.*, pp. 224–25. It is perhaps difficult to regard this statement of the relativity of the content of morality as much more than a flight of rhetoric. However, it is quite possible that, with some slight qualification, Voltaire means exactly what he says here. Although he would not approve of breaking one's word without an unusual reason, he seems to look with some degree of equanimity upon the Spartan encouragement of adultery, upon polygamy, and even upon the Roman tolerance of a father's slaying his own children.

[4] *Ibid.*, pp. 225–26. Some years later, Voltaire denies that one can act in any manner other than as he pleases, unless he is physically incapacitated. This would mean, then, that the virtuous man is one who finds it pleasing to himself to please others; he is not, however, any more free to determine what shall please him than the planets are to determine their courses through the heavens.

mouth, laws by which I wish you to govern yourselves"; rather, God has given men certain instincts comparable to those of the social insects. These instincts are certain feelings of which man can never completely divest himself; they are the eternal bonds and first laws of human society foreseen by God.[5] One of these instincts is the feeling of benevolence (*bienveillance*) which is innate in man and is always active, unless, of course, it be overcome by self-love (*amour-propre*). That is, every man feels inclined to assist another who is in need—as long as it does not cost him anything to do so.[6] Even a savage dripping with the blood of enemies on whom he has just feasted will come to the aid of his comrade in need.

Though adultery and homosexuality are permitted among many people, Voltaire asserts, there is no country in which the failure to keep one's word is regarded favorably. This is quite understandable, for society can subsist amid adultery and homosexuality, but not if the citizens deceive one another.[7] Theft, too, is in a sense evil in all societies; that is, once the custom of private ownership has been established, thievery is unjust. If, however, a society were to consider it advisable, that is, suitable to its needs, to abolish the custom of private property, then stealing would no longer be a vice. The good of society is the sole criterion by which one can judge what is just or unjust. In fact, even lying is on occasion so clearly required by the circumstances that telling the truth would constitute a vice.[8]

In the *Dictionary* article, "Amour nommé Socratique," Voltaire rejects the notion that homosexuality could be regarded as moral

---

[5] In virtue of what Voltaire has said elsewhere about man's inability to understand the divine prescience and in virtue also of Voltaire's ultimate denial of the possibility of such foreknowledge in God, it is strange that the *philosophe* adduces here that same prescience as an explanation of the similarities of all systems of law. A further appeal to the divine foreknowledge is made when Voltaire notes that it is the nature of men to make war upon one another. Because God has foreseen this, he says, God has arranged that there be more boys than girls born each year. *Traité*, Moland, XXII, 228.

[6] *Ibid.*, p. 226. "Ainsi un homme est toujours porté à assister un autre homme quand il ne lui en coûte rien."

[7] *Ibid.*

[8] *Ibid.*, pp. 226–27. Voltaire's willingness, on pragmatic grounds, to tolerate adultery, homosexuality, and absolute community of property in a state is evidence, it would seem, of a very superficial appreciation of man's psychic needs, a reduction of human requirements to the most elementary animal satisfactions.

in any society, that it is not contrary to a universal moral law. He writes:

> Sextus Empiricus and others have said in vain that pederasty was recommended by the laws of Persia. Let them cite the text of the law; let them point out the code of the Persians; and even if they point it out, I will still not believe it. I will say the thing is not true, because it is impossible. No, it is not in human nature to make a law which contradicts and outrages human nature, a law which would annihilate the human race if it were observed to the letter. How many people have taken the shameful and tolerated customs of a country for the laws of the country! [9]

Voltaire's reference to homosexuality as a "shameful custom" need not be due so much to a change of mind with the passage of the years as to a failure on Voltaire's part to reconcile two contradictory positions. On the one hand, he never quite succeeded in eliminating his common sense conviction that there is an "ought" stemming from man's nature; on the other hand, his deterministic philosophy left no room for an "ought," but only for the inevitable, necessary consequences of the eternal divine causality. If man is not truly free in his choices, there is no reason for referring to any custom as "shameful."

If one is impelled by such an explanation of the nature and origin of morality to protest that it is a complete relativism, denying that there is anything good in itself independently of man, Voltaire has anticipated the objection and answered it. The quality of morality or immorality, he says, has no more objective reality than temperature, texture, and odor. Just as no one would dream that heat and cold exist in themselves, so no one should imagine that virtue and vice are anything other than completely relative to man. Anyone who would assert that health and sickness have no reality except as related to man should also be willing to grant that morality and immorality are just as much modifications of man and not subsistent beings. This Voltairian argument, however,

---

[9] "Amour nommé Socratique" (1764), *D.P.*, Naves, p. 20. "Sextus Empiricus et d'autres ont beau dire que la pédérastie était recommandée par les lois de la Perse. Qu'ils citent le texte de la loi; qu'ils montrent le code des Persans, et, s'ils le montrent, je ne le croirai pas encore, je dirai que la chose n'est pas vraie, par la raison qu'elle est impossible. Non, il n'est pas dans la nature humaine de faire une loi qui contredit et qui outrage la nature, une loi qui anéantirait le genre humain si elle était observée à la lettre. Que de gens ont pris des usages honteux et tolérés dans un pays pour les lois du pays!"

appears to confuse the question: relativity of morals is not opposed to a subsistent morality in such a manner that one must
choose one of the two positions. A common natural basis of morality could stem from an unchanging human nature, the nature itself being a criterion of what is useful or fitting for all men at all
times and places. Another alternative to a relativistic morality is
the opinion that God has imposed upon man a system of laws to
be observed universally and forever, either because such laws are
required by human nature or simply because they are the laws
that God wills man to observe.

Moreover, Voltaire has himself posited at least some natural law,
when he says that man's social nature requires that every man
obey whatever laws there are in his state, and again when he says
that truth, gratitude, and friendliness are regarded everywhere as
marks of the virtuous man. Also, in Voltaire's concept of man's position in the universe, a very important thesis is that God has decreed the nature of man and the physical laws to which he is subject and that man should, therefore, be content with what the
divine will has determined for him. It would seem, then, that, despite his professed relativism in ethics, Voltaire admitted at least
one thesis from each of the aforesaid systems of common and per-
manent morality.

Voltaire considers the case of the man who rejects the notion
that he must obey the laws of his society, the man who says that,
if it suits his own purposes, he will murder, steal, and abandon
himself completely to his passions. It is precisely for such people
as this, Voltaire says, that laws are made. Such a man will court de-
struction, for just as wolves that prey upon sheep are killed, so a
citizen who preys upon his countrymen will be destroyed by the
authorities. Therefore, it would not be truly advantageous for a
citizen to act in such a lawless manner. Even if such a man had an
army at his command, he could not violate the laws of society
with impunity; he would soon learn that chastisement is inescapable: either he would receive the chastisement men so wisely mete
out to the enemies of society (Voltaire does not say what these
chastisements are) or he would be sufficiently punished by the
very fear of punishment. It is morally impossible that a bad man
not be recognized for what he is; and, from the moment that he
is so recognized, he is regarded with suspicion and disgust. Further, God has so made men that they cannot endure living among
others who distrust and despise them. It is God-given pride which

is the best guarantee that every man will consider it to be to his own advantage to obey the laws of society, even though he be persuaded that virtue and vice are of no consequence.[10]

The same ideas were expressed in the earlier *Remarques sur les Pensées de M. Pascal:*

> It is as impossible that a society should be formed and endure without self-love as it is that children should be begotten without concupiscence or that one should eat without an appetite. It is the love of self that enables one to love others; it is by reason of our mutual needs that we are useful to mankind; it is the foundation of all commerce; it is the eternal bond uniting men. Without self-love no art would ever have been invented, nor would there ever have been a society of as many as ten persons. It is this self-love which every animal has received from nature which warns us to respect that of others. Law directs this self-love; religion perfects it. It is quite true that God could have made creatures uniquely attentive to the good of others, and in this case merchants would have gone to the Indies out of charity and masons would cut stone in order to please their neighbor. But God has established things otherwise. Let us never despise the instinct he has given us, but use it according to his command.[11]

Having reduced virtue and vice to a level of enlightened self-interest, Voltaire then proceeds to note that great men such as Bayle, Locke, Spinoza, Shaftesbury, and Collins were the most virtuous of men, not because they feared the disapproval of their fellow men, but solely because they had a taste for virtue itself. Then, having cast doubt upon the desirability of what he has just

---

[10] *Traité*, Moland, XXII, 228–29. In the *Homélies*, "Sur l'Athéisme" (1765), Moland, XXVI, 323, it is said that nature punishes the evil-doer, but Voltaire does not in this place explain how this is accomplished.

[11] *Remarques sur les Pensées de M. Pascal*, Moland, XXII, 36–37: "Il est aussi impossible qu'une société puisse se former et subsister sans amour-propre qu'il serait impossible de faire des enfants sans concupiscence, de songer à se nourrir sans appétit. C'est l'amour de nous-mêmes qui assiste l'amour des autres; c'est par nos besoins mutuels que nous sommes utiles au genre humain, c'est le fondement de tout commerce; c'est l'éternel lien des hommes. Sans lui il n'y aurait pas eu un art inventé, ni une société de dix personnes formée. C'est cet amour-propre que chaque animal a reçu de la nature, qui nous avertit de respecter celui des autres. La loi dirige cet amour-propre, et la religion le perfectionne. Il est vrai que Dieu aurait pu faire des créatures uniquement attentives au bien d'autres. Dans ce cas les merchands auraient été aux Indes par charité, le maçon scié de la pierre pour faire plaisir à son prochain, etc. Mais Dieu a établi les choses autrement: n'accusons point l'instinct qu'il nous donne, et faisons-en l'usage qu'il commande."

posited as man's God-given guarantee of civil obedience, namely fear of being despised by one's fellow citizens, Voltaire declares that this admirable taste for virtue in the above-mentioned men has the same sort of cause as a cultivated taste for fine wines. Just as a proprer education trains men to prefer fine wines, so a proper education trains men to be "honorable," to prefer virtue to vice. Finally, Voltaire makes one last *volte-face* back to a natural foundation for virtue and observes that those who find it necessary to have religious motives for being virtuous are monsters, for their virtue, instead of being the effect of a natural cause, is founded on something unnatural.[12]

True religion, however, is not unnatural; there is a certain kind of recognition and service of the deity which is incumbent upon all men. In the *Elements of Newton's Philosophy* Voltaire points out that Newton did not think that man had any innate ideas, sentiments, or principles. Rather, Newton thought that God had given to all men the same senses, and, as a consequence of this, all men have the same needs, acquire the same sentiments, and develop the same generalized notions which are everywhere the foundations of society and the content of natural religion. For this reason, truth, gratitude, and friendliness are held from Siam to Mexico to be marks of the good man, the religious man. Natural religion is identical with the moral principles which are common to all men.[13]

Voltaire remarks, however, that Locke, for all his sagacity, went to extremes when he took the position that there are no notions of good and evil common to all men. Had he been a bit more cautious in accepting as true the reports brought back to England by travelers who observed carelessly, were ignorant of the native languages, and mistook for law what was actually a violation of it, then Locke would not have been deceived into believing that there were actually nations among which it was an approved custom to eat one's own children or to practice bestiality. Voltaire himself would not be so easily deceived. If, he says, he were told that in certain countries the inhabitants eat their aged parents

---

[12] *Traité*, Moland, XXII, 229. It is in passages like those just considered that one feels that what is expressed is not nearly so much a reasoned argument as it is the tempestuous, prejudiced, and flippant personality of Voltaire. It is a variety of philosophical expressionism.

[13] *Eléments*, Moland, XXII, 419. "J'entends par religion naturelle les principes de morale commune au genre humain."

from a motive of piety, he would either doubt the truth of the story or he would interpret the practice as a barbaric manner of showing respect towards one's parents, a manner which would be, however, a horrible abuse of a natural law. Nonetheless, if the deed were done from a desire to provide for the parents a final resting place within a filial breast, then, frightful though it may be to the imagination, it would be a consequence of kindheartedness, an act of natural religion.[14]

Natural religion is nothing other than that law which is known throughout the entire universe: do unto others as you would have them do unto you. This, of course, involves working for the common good in society. In fact, Voltaire is so certain that this is the essence of natural religion that he is prepared to deny there is such a thing as natural religion, should anyone be able to find for him a society of ten or more persons in which what is conducive to the common good is not esteemed. In the ancient society in which thievery was looked upon with favor, it was so regarded precisely because thievery was thought to be conducive to the common good. That is, there was to be no private property, and anyone who appropriated goods for himself was properly punished by having them taken from him. Such thievery was then an act of natural religion.[15] When Locke says that men have different ideas of justice, he means only that there are different forms of natural religion, different ideas of justice; he means only that there are different ways of carrying out the injunction to do to others what one would like done to himself. All other rules of so-

---

[14] *Ibid.*, p. 420. Voltaire's interpretation of Locke on the question of the universality of law is subject to criticism. See Locke, *Essay on Human Understanding*, I, ii, 13 (Fraser edition, I, 78): "I would not be here mistaken, as if, because I deny an innate law, I thought there were none but positive laws. There is a great deal of difference between an innate law, and a law of nature; between something imprinted on our minds in their very original, and something that we, being ignorant of, may attain to the knowledge of, by the use and due application of our natural faculties."

[15] *Eléments*, Moland, XXII, 421. For another explanation of "natural religion," see *Entretiens chinois* (1770), Moland, XXVII, 32–34, and *Profession de foi des Théistes* (1768), Moland, XXVII, 55–58. In the *Idées de La Mothe le Vayer* (1751), Moland, XXIII, 490, Voltaire had described natural religion: "What is the religion which can do good and cannot do evil? Is it not the adoration of a supreme being, without any metaphysical dogma? That which would be within the reach of all men? That which stripped of all superstition, separated from all deceit, would be content to render solemn thanks to God without attempting to penetrate into his secrets?"

ciety can be reduced to this one, and Locke certainly does not mean to deny this or to assert that God has not given to all men their instinctive self-love which guides them with an irresistible necessity.[16]

What Locke wished to teach, Voltaire assures us, was that there is in man no innate "conscience," which infallibly informs him what is just and what is unjust. Ideas of justice and good principles must be instilled into the mind when it begins to use its faculties. It is these ideas and principles, created in man by the spirit of his age, by example, and by his own dispositions and reflections, that make up whatever conscience he has. "Man is born without any [moral] principles, but he has the faculty of receiving all of them." [17] Depending upon his natural disposition, he will be inclined either to cruelty or kindness; his reason will indicate to him that he ought not do to others what he would not have done to himself. While this natural disposition influences him from his very birth, the judgment that expresses the "golden rule" will become evident to him only as he becomes mature. A child acts mechanically and often in a manner entirely contrary to the "eternal principle" embodied in this rule. The parents of the child, however, educate him in such a manner that he becomes social; and it is this education which bestows a conscience on him. This conscience becomes so strong in those properly educated that, from the age of seven to sixteen or seventeen, they cannot perform a single evil action without being reproached by their conscience.[18]

---

[16] In his *Leningrad Notebook*, however, Voltaire distinguishes between self-love and benevolence. He writes: "It would seem that nature has given us self-love for our own conservation, and benevolence for the conservation of others; and perhaps without these two principles, of which the first ought to be the stronger, there could be no society at all." *Voltaire's Notebooks*, I, 219.

[17] "Conscience" (1771), *Q.E.*, Moland, XVIII, 235: "L'homme n'est né avec aucun principe [morale], mais avec la faculté de les recevoir tous."

[18] *Ibid.* "Ensuite viennent les violentes passions qui combattent la conscience, et qui l'étouffent quelquefois." See also the Piccini Notebook, *Voltaire's Notebooks*, II, 390: "La religion naturelle peut suffire contre les crimes qu'on commet seul et en secret; car la nature donne des remords." Just exactly how remorse is a consequence of one's having acted in a manner contrary to a rule that one has adopted as a purely pragmatic measure is difficult to explain; even acting in a manner contrary to parental and social conditioning would seem to be productive of remorse only if there were a presupposition that one *ought* not act in such a manner.

In an article published in 1767, Voltaire writes that there is only one morality, just as there is only one geometry.[19] While it is true that not everyone knows geometry, nevertheless, if one applies himself to the study of the subject, he will come to agree with the thought of all other geometers. In the field of morality it is the same; those who consider the matter carefully all come to the same conclusions about justice and injustice. Confucius did not construct a system of morality as one constructs a physical system; he found it in the heart of all men. Morality has nothing to do with dogma; dogmas differ, but morality is everywhere the same among men who use their reason. One can conclude, then, that morality must come from God.[20] In the *Cambridge Notebook* the same thing is repeated: No one disputes about the essence of religon, which is to do good; disputes concern only unintelligible dogmas. If religion were content to say, "Be just," there would be no unbelievers on earth.[21] Men would not dispute about the nature of the just and unjust. Morality is the same everywhere and unchangeable; it comes from God. It is he who has given men the ability to know, as soon as they know that two and two make four, that there are vice and virtue. Man's principles of reason and morality will be eternally the same, for they come from the eternally immutable God. They come, however, not as innate ideas or feelings; they are *acquired* by all men, who have the same senses and receive the same ideas by means of these senses.[22]

In still another attempt to clarify Locke's position, or perhaps to make it conform to Voltaire's own convictions, the latter had written to Crown Prince Frederick that Locke is reasonable in combating the theory of innate moral ideas, but that he goes too

---

[19] One is led to wonder what effect the non-Euclidean geometries would have had on Voltaire's thinking.

[20] "Morale" (1767), *D.P.*, Naves, pp. 325–26. Voltaire does not state here what he considers to be the content of this universal morality.

[21] *Voltaire's Notebooks*, I, 52. Norman Torrey makes an interesting observation concerning the relationship Voltaire posited between religion and morality. "It is this belief in a universal morality 'as old as creation,' that lies at the bottom of the deistic movement. 'Religion should be in conformity with morality,' Voltaire wrote, 'and universal like morality; thus every religion whose dogmas offend morality is certainly false.' If he had let Christianity alone, if he had called his universal morality a 'categorical imperative' as did Kant, and had built a nebulous philosophical system upon it, he would be revered today as Kant is revered. He chose the more difficult and the more dangerous course and laid himself open to the charge that attacks on religion do not constitute a philosophy." *The Spirit of Voltaire*, 229–30.

[22] "Du juste et de l'injuste" (1765), *D.P.*, Naves, pp. 269–70.

far if he presumes to deny that there is any universal moral principle. While it is true that man is not born with any moral proposition in his soul, yet God has so formed human organs that all men, at a certain age, come to acquire the ideas of justice and injustice. It is something like the fact that all men who are born with two legs will one day be able to walk, though no one expects a new-born child to do so. It is true that different customs will result in various nations' attaching different meanings to the idea of justice, so that what is a crime in Europe may be considered virtue in Asia.[23] Nevertheless, what is good for society is the immutable rule of virtue; what is useful to society is regarded as good in all countries.[24]

While in his earlier writings there is no evidence that Voltaire regarded a belief in God as exercising any influence on one's moral actions, or even regarded such belief as having anything to do with religion, which he reduced to the "golden rule," there are some thoughts expressed in the *Piccini Notebook* (1750–1755), which indicate a new viewpoint on the subject:

> Religion is good only insofar as it admits principles on which everyone agrees, just as a law is good only if it effects the security of all levels of society. Therefore, we ought to leave to religion whatever is useful for all men and eliminate everything else. It is useful to all society that its members believe in a just God and that they act justly; it is useful that there be temples where God is adored, his benefits hymned, his justice declared, and virtue recommended. Whatever goes beyond this . . . ought to be proscribed.[25]

---

[23] As Voltaire writes in *Le Philosophe ignorant* (1766), Moland, XXVI, 85, though there is one fundamental law of morality, there are a thousand different interpretations of this one law in a thousand different circumstances. In his *Remarques pour servir de supplément à l'Essai sur les moeurs et l'esprit des nations*, Moland, XXIV, 573, he notes that it is opinion, a kind of guesswork, which has made civil law. As a consequence laws are ambiguous, insufficient, and contradictory. It is not the fact that laws have been drawn up by men that makes them so inadequate, for geometry, physics, and metaphysics have also been formulated by men, and these sciences embody unchangeable truths. What constitutes the difference is that laws have been passed to take care of transient needs or to provide a medicine which may, by luck, cure one portion of society, but by a less fortunate chance, doom another class. It remains, however, that the fundamental principle of such guesswork is the good of society.

[24] Letter of c. October 15, 1737, *Correspondence*, Besterman, VI, 227–28.

[25] *Voltaire's Notebooks*, II, 375. "La religion n'est bonne qu'autant qu'elle admet des principes dont tout le monde convient; de même qu'une loi n'est bonne qu'autant qu'elle fait la sûreté de tous les ordres de l'état: donc il

It makes no difference whether the unthinking common people have truths or errors given them, wisdom or foolishness; they will follow one equally as well as the other; they are only a blind machine. It is not so with those people who think. . . . They begin by doubting an absurd legend, and, unfortunately, take the legend for religion. Then they say, "There is no religion at all," and abandon themselves to crime.[26]

There is obviously a causal connection here between a denial of religion and an abandonment to a life of immorality.

Though there is no certitude that Voltaire has in mind here a religion involving belief in God, in the *Philosophical Dictionary* there are some passages which indicate clearly that he did at one period regard religion, understood in the theistic sense, as an important moral force, at least for the common people. In the article, "God," Voltaire addresses Holbach: "You fear that adoring God will quickly make one superstitious and fanatical again; but ought one not rather fear that denying God will bring one to abandoning oneself to one's passions, to the most atrocious and frightful crimes?" [27] There is, nonetheless, the possibility that Voltaire is again, in combating an opponent, making use of a proposi-

---

faut laisser à la religion ce qui est utile à tous les hommes, et retrancher tout le reste.—Il est utile à toute société que l'on croie un dieu juste, et qu'on soit juste: il est utile qu'il y ait des temples où dieu soit adoré, ses bienfaits chantés, sa justice annoncée, la vertu recommandée; ce qui est au-delà . . . doit être proscrit."

[26] *Ibid.*, p. 391. "Il est égal pour le peuple non pensant qu'on lui donne des vérités ou des erreurs à croire, de la sagesse ou de la folie; il suivra également l'un ou l'autre: il n'est que machine aveugle. Il n'en est pas ainsi du peuple pensant . . . il commence par douter d'une légende absurde, et malheureusement cette légende est prise par lui pour la religion; alors il dit: Il n'y a point de religion, et il s'abandonne au crime."

It is difficult to understand how Voltaire ever came to be regarded by the French Revolutionaries as a hero, as a defender of the rights of man. In the light of his comments on the "common man," one can only suggest, by way of explanation, that the Revolutionaries regarded the Church and the oppressive upper classes as allies of each other and thought that Voltaire, because he attacked the Church, was an enemy of the upper classes and a friend of the "common man." It is quite evident that Constance Rowe, in her *Voltaire and the State* (New York: Columbia University Press, 1955), pp. 93–133, was hard put to it to find any evidence of democracy in Voltaire. Her attempt to prove Voltaire a democrat involves not much more than pointing out his objections to clerical authority.

[27] "Dieu," *Q.E.*, Naves, p. 519. "Vous craignez 'qu'en adorant Dieu on ne redevienne bientôt superstitieux et fanatique'; mais n'est-il pas à craindre qu'en le niant on ne s'abandonne aux passions les plus atroces et aux crimes les plus affreux?"

tion he does not truely hold. However, it is not so easy to dismiss a question directed to Bayle, who had stated that it was possible for men not to believe in God and still to live in society: "When you have lent your money to someone in your society, would you wish that neither your debtor, nor your lawyer, nor your notary, nor your judge believed in God?"[28]

It is a most interesting question, Voltaire notes, whether it is better for men to believe in a God who rewards and punishes, who makes recompense for hidden actions, both good and bad, than not so to believe.[29] To answer this question, however, it is necessary to make a distinction between the philosophers and the common people. It is very true that in every country the populace requires a very strong rein; in fact, if Bayle had had even as many as five or six hundred peasants to govern, he would have lost no time in declaring to them that there is a God who rewards and punishes. For the philosophical, though, no such sanction is required. Where there is question, however, of *savage* nations, asking the people whether they believe in God or not is like asking them whether they are for Aristotle or Democritus: they understand as much about the one as about the other.[30]

In an article in the *Questions on the Encyclopedia*, Voltaire states rather more clearly his conviction that belief in God is a deterrent from evil. It is a fact, he says, that the great criminals at the head of governments and their subordinate officers have not believed in God at all. What resource have we left, then, against robbery, contemptuousness, outrage, calumny, and persecution? That of convincing the strong man who oppresses the weak that there is a God.[31] In yet another place, Voltaire writes unambiguously that it is clear that, from the standpoint of morality, it is

---

[28] "Athée, Athéisme" (1770), *Q.E.*, Naves, p. 459. "Je vous demanderai toujours si, quand vous avez prêté votre argent à quelqu'un de votre société, vous voudriez que ni votre débiteur, ni votre procureur, ni votre notaire, ni votre juge, ne crussent en Dieu."

[29] In the *A.B.C.* (1762), Moland, XXVII, 400, Voltaire had even suggested that it would be desirable to abandon his philosophical conclusion that all that exists or happens, exists and happens necessarily, if it should appear that such a position would adversely affect morality by its corollary that there is nothing in man's actions which deserves punishment.

[30] "Athée, Athéisme" (1770), *Q.E.*, Naves, p. 459. The last statement reveals one more inconsistency in Voltaire's thinking; when he is attempting to prove the existence of God, he states that even the savage knows from his observations of nature that there is a supreme being.

[31] "Eucharistie" (1771), *Q.E.*, Moland, XIX, 39.

more preferable to admit that there is a God rather than deny it. It is without doubt in the interest of all men that there should be a divine being who will punish what human justice is not able to restrain.[32] Again, in the *Dictionary*,

> I should not like to have to deal with an atheistic prince who would find it to his own interest to have me ground to powder in a mortar. I am quite sure that I should be so ground. Nor would I wish, if I were a ruler, to deal with atheistic courtiers who would find it in their interest to poison me. I might have to take antidotes every day. It is, therefore, absolutely necessary for both prince and people that the idea of a supreme being, creator, governor, rewarder, and punisher be deeply engraved on all hearts.[33]

In the *Dictionary* article on "Fraud" there is a dialogue between a fakir, Brambabef, and a Confucian named Wang. Brambabef asserts that it is good to deceive the people, for God himself has done this very thing in making it necessary that man see the sun in such a way that it appears to have a diameter of two or three feet, the stars and the moon as if they were equally distant from the earth, and a square tower as round from a distance. Therefore, it is admirable to deceive the citizenry with myths, pretended miracles, and the like, which will inspire them to a desirable degree of morality. Wang objects that the best manner of assuring that a citizenry will be just is to inspire them with a natural religion, a religion without superstition. There is no need of miracles to persuade the people that there is a just God who reads their hearts and metes out punishments and rewards. Indeed, Wang has seen villages in which these two propositions, that God exists and that he rewards and punishes, constituted the whole of their religion, and in which there was greater virtue than in any other village he had seen. Brambabef, still not convinced, objects that the philosophers will not admit the existence of an

---

[32] "Athée," *D.P.*, Moland, XVII, 455. (Beuchot estimates that this article was written between 1765 and 1770. See Moland, XVII, viii–ix.)

[33] "Athée, Athéisme" (1770), *D.P.*, Naves, p. 43. "Je ne voudrais pas avoir affaire à un prince athée, qui trouverait son intérêt à me faire piler dans un mortier: je suis bien sûr que je serais pilé. Je ne voudrais pas, si j'étais souverain, avoir affaire à des courtisans athées, dont l'intérêt serait de m'empoisonner: il me faudrait prendre au hasard du contrepoison tous les jours. Il est donc absolument nécessaire pour les princes et pour les peuples, que l'idée d'un Etre suprême, créateur, gouverneur, rémunérateur et vengeur, soit profondément gravée dans les esprits."

avenging God. No matter, explains Wang, the philosophers will also be virtuous men; it is, in fact, better to be virtuous from love, as are the philosophers, than from fear, as are the common people. Moreover, no philosopher can be *sure* that God will not reward and punish. Upon being convinced that a purely natural religion is sufficient to insure morality in society, Brambabef is converted to Confucianism.[34]

The same sort of distinction between what is useful for the common man and what is useful for the philosopher appears in the *Philosophical Dictionary* article on "Hell." We are, says Voltaire, obliged to transact affairs with villains who are not too intelligent, with persons addicted to brutality, drunkenness, rapaciousness; our dealings are not all with a Cicero or a Marcus Aurelius or a Newton. Therefore, while others may, if they please, tell the unphilosophical and vicious that the soul is not immortal and there is no hell, Voltaire himself will thunder in their ears that they will certainly be damned if they do not deal justly with *him*. What would be the state of affairs in London, he asks, if everyone were convinced there is no hell? What restraint would there be upon evil? Only the restraint of honor, of the laws, and of God, who wills that men be just, regardless of whether there is a hell. Such restraints, however, will not do for the lower levels of society.[35]

Bernard N. Schilling, in his *Conservative England and the Case against Voltaire*, calls attention to the conclusions which must be drawn from Voltaire's statements about the usefulness of teaching the common people that there is a God who will punish in hell those who are unjust: either it is true that there is such a God and such punishment does await the sinner, or God has so constructed the universe that the good order of society depends

---

[34] "Fraude" (1764), *D.P.*, Naves, pp. 207–11. Brambabef has not, however, been converted to the extent of a Pauline enthusiasm: he requests Wang not to inform the other fakirs of his conversion.

[35] "Enfer" (1772), *Q.E.*, Moland, XVIII, 548. Only the philosophers are truly religious; that is, only they truly recognize God and are virtuous. "Sur dix millions il y a tout au plus cinq mille pensants, et sur vingt millions dix mille: parmi ces dix mille, il n'y a pas cinquante personnes d'accord. Ainsi la multitude sera toujours composée de brutes." See Piccini Notebook, *Voltaire's Notebooks*, II, 405. The multitude, therefore, being made up of brutes, must be restrained by being told that evil-doers will be punished in hell. See also Daniel Mornet, *Les origines intellectuelles de la Révolution française (1715–1787)* (Paris: A. Colin, 1933), pp. 86–87, for Voltaire's contemptuous attitude toward the common man.

upon the perpetuation of a lie.[36] It is extremely difficult to believe that Voltaire would have granted the latter part of the dichotomy; but it is equally difficult to think that he would have granted the former. Possibly Voltaire simply failed to see the consequences of his principles, or possibly he would dehorn the dilemma by arguing that the good order of society does not depend upon the perpetuation of a lie among the enlightened, but only among the common people, who are not worthy of serious consideration.

Unfortunately, it is not possible to summarize Voltaire's ethical thought without noting some discrepancies. At one time Voltaire appears to think that self-love is the sole driving force of human nature; at another, he grants a second force, benevolence, a natural inclination to assist others. While he asserts in one place that it makes no difference what the laws of a country are, that the only important thing is that they be obeyed, in other places he explains why certain acts are regarded as virtuous or vicious by all men. It may very well be that Norman Torrey is correct when he states that the rational Voltaire was dominated by the "mystical Voltaire" on occasion, and this domination resulted in an attempt to portray moral laws as being as uniform and unchangeable as the laws of physics.[37] Had Voltaire been consistently the empiricist, he would have maintained consistently his doctrine of moral relativism. Not, however, that his moral relativism, as Torrey points out, was something totally unrelated to justice; rather, the man-made laws to which the good man must conform would have been impossible without a concept of justice. Nonetheless, if one takes very seriously Voltaire's statement that laws are made for the very people who would otherwise have no regard for others, this justice, arising from common human instincts and common human needs rooted in a common physical structure, seems to be only an effect of self-interest, somewhat in the fashion of a Hobbesian agreement to end the war of all against all.

In the passages in which Voltaire appeals to the good of society as the norm of morality, there is no indication that he had given

---

[36] Bernard N. Schilling, *Conservative England and the Case against Voltaire* (New York: Columbia University Press, 1950), p. 190. Peter Gay, in his *Voltaire's Politics* (Princeton: Princeton University Press, 1959), points out the contradiction in Voltaire's thought on this question: "Voltaire continually affirms that men must be told the truth, and continually praises the efficacy of lies." P. 265.

[37] Norman Torrey, *The Spirit of Voltaire*, p. 260.

much reflection to the question of what *is* the good of society. He has never, for example, coped with the problem of whether the good of society is merely the collective good of its members, a good proper to society as such and superior to the good of the individual, or a good proper to society as such but ordered ultimately to the good of the individual. A further difficulty lies in the fact that such a norm will not function where there is question of actions which have no discernible effect on society.

In short, it must be acknowledged that Voltaire's ethical writing is either ambiguous or reflects an indecision in the *philosophe's* own mind. The latter alternative is quite possible in view of the fact that Voltaire drew at various times upon the writings of such varied authors as Mandeville, Locke, and Newton. Moreover, it would seem that one who rejects human freedom, in the sense of the ability to determine oneself, is attempting an impossible task when he assays to construct a genuine philosophy of morality, for morality is concerned primarily, not with what *is*, but with what *ought to be*. And "ought" can have no meaning for men who are as completely determined by natural laws as are the inanimate things of the material universe.

Voltaire's attempt to portray man as a member of society does not, then, introduce any drastic change into the Voltairian notion of the material universe as operating according to unchangeable, mathematical laws. What Voltaire's ethical philosophy does introduce is a note of uneasiness in its author as he struggles to give meaning to ethical statements without denying the metaphysical principles from which his determinism stems.

Having considered that term of the relationship between God and the universe which can be studied empirically, we shall proceed to an analysis of Voltaire's position with regard to the other term, God.

CHAPTER SIX

The Existence of God

So INSEPARABLY connected with his philosophy of the material universe are Voltaire's theological speculations that, as has been seen, he is unable to treat the former without bringing into his arguments presuppositions or conclusions from the latter. That is, Voltaire found it impossible to treat philosophically of the sensible universe without noting its relation to God. Skeptical though the *philosophe* was concerning anything like a divine revelation of God to man, he gives only the slightest reason for suspecting that he ever doubted the existence of a supreme being. This slight reason is so overwhelmingly offset by his reiterated and varied arguments in favor of God's existence that it is impossible to classify Voltaire as an atheist or to assert reasonably that his private opinion on the matter was quite different from his public pronouncements.[1]

In each of his important philosophical works, Voltaire considered the question of the existence of God, and in each of them he concluded that the evidence was sufficient to warrant an affirmation. To understand his position, then, it seems necessary to study the arguments Voltaire elaborated in the *Treatise on Metaphysics* and the *Elements of Newton's Philosophy*, in both of which there is an extended treatment of the problem, and in his later works, which deal with the question in a more summary manner. Also, inasmuch as the question was raised by Voltaire himself, as well as by some of his commentators, some consideration must be given to the certitude of the Voltairian arguments.

In what is perhaps his earliest extended passage on the question

---

[1] Voltaire suffered, in fact, some humiliation in the circle of Frederick's philosophical friends, because the Frenchman maintained his theistic position. It was said of him, "Voltaire est bigot, il est déiste," and Holbach scornfully remarked that a man who would accept the existence of God would accept *anything*. See Alfred Noyes, *Voltaire* (New York: Sheed and Ward, 1936), p. 426.

of the existence of God, Voltaire takes up, in the *Treatise on Metaphysics*, the Cartesian argument that an idea of God is natural to man. If, he says, such an idea belongs to human nature, then it is impossible to explain how there are barbarians who simply do not have such an idea; nor is it any easier to explain how tribes such as the Hottentots should have an idea of God so totally different from that of more civilized peoples. Similarly, there are among civilized peoples children who, though they often pronounce the word, "God," never come to understand its meaning. This, of course, raises a problem. If one maintains that an idea of God is not a property of human nature and yet acknowledges what can scarcely be denied, namely, that all men are born with five fingers on each hand and with a nose, then it seems to follow that it is more important to have the requisite number of digits and an olfactory organ than to have a knowledge of God. Deplorable though this arrangement may be, Voltaire answers, it is certainly the situation in which man finds himself. Nevertheless, there are two ways in which man *can* arrive at some knowledge of God.[2]

The more natural and the simpler of these two ways begins with a consideration of the order in the universe, together with the end to which each thing seems to be ordered. Many ponderous volumes have been written on this subject, but their content can all be condensed into this simple argument: when one sees a watch one must conclude to the existence of an intelligent being who has arranged its works in such wise that the hands will indicate the hour. Similarly, when one observes the human body with all its intricate organs, one can only acknowledge that an intelligent being has arranged them and ordered the various parts toward their end, that is, the eye toward seeing, the hands toward grasping objects, etc. From these observations, however, one can conclude only that an intelligent and superior being has skillfully prepared and fashioned matter; one is not entitled to argue from the facts that this being also made the matter or that he is in every sense infinite.[3]

---

[2] *Traité*, Moland, XXII, 194.

[3] *Ibid*. Other expressions of the argument from finality and the intricate design of living things can be found in: *Extrait de la Bibliothèque raisonnée* (c. 1752), Moland, XXIII, 535–36; *Dialogues entre Lucrèce et Posidonius* (1756), Moland, XXIV, 57–69; *Homélies*, "Sur Athéisme" (1765), Moland, XXVI, 316; and *Il faut prendre un parti* (1772), Moland, XXVIII, 549. In the last-named, Voltaire writes: "Personne ne doute qu'une sphère armillaire, des paysages, des animaux dessinés, des anatomies en cire colorée, ne

The second argument is a more metaphysical one, and therefore less capable of being understood by duller minds; it is, however, more fruitful, capable of leading to a wider knowledge. Since I exist, something exists. If something exists, something has existed from all eternity; for a being exists either by reason of itself or because it has received its being from another. If a being exists by reason of itself, then it exists necessarily; it has always existed; it is God. If a being has received its existence from another, and this second being from a third, and so on, the being from which the last in the series has received its existence must necessarily be God. It is only God who can create, and it is inconceivable that one being should give existence to another without having the power of creating. Moreover, if one says that a being received, not its form, but its existence from another, and that other from a third, and the third from a further being, and so on *ad infinitum*, one is speaking nonsense, for then no being in the series would have any cause of its existence. Taken as a whole, the series would have no external cause of existence; taken individually, the beings would have no internal cause of their existence. That is, taken collectively they would owe their existence to nothing; taken distributively none of them would exist by reason of itself, and therefore none would exist necessarily. Consequently, one is led to avow that there is a being which exists necessarily, by reason of itself, for all eternity, a being which is the source of all other beings. From this it follows that this being is infinite in duration, in immensity, in power.[4]

If a materialist, however, objects that these characteristics are precisely the ones he attributes to matter, that is, that matter is self-existent, necessary, eternal, infinite in duration, extent, and power, then the contradictions of his own theory must be pointed out to him. If the material universe exists necessarily, then it

---

soient des ouvrages d'artistes habiles. Se pourrait-il que les copies fussent d'une intelligence, et que les originaux n'en fussent pas? Cette seule idée me paraît la plus forte démonstration, et je ne conçois pas comment on peut la combattre." Voltaire is repeating here an argument which Samuel Clarke had used to prove the existence of God. See *A Demonstration of the Being and Attributes of God* (8th ed., London: J. J. Knapton, 1732), pp. 68–69. Voltaire does not follow Clarke, however, on the question of the creation of matter, nor on that of the infinity of God. *Ibid.*, pp. 73–80. For an analysis of the proofs offered by Clarke, see Richard H. Luecke, *God and Contingency in the Philosophies of Locke, Clarke, and Leibniz* (Thesis: University of Chicago, 1955).

[4] *Traité*, Moland, XXII, 194–95.

would be contradictory to suppose that the tiniest part of it could be otherwise than it now is; that is, if what exists at this moment exists with an absolute necessity, then any other mode of being is excluded, and all change is impossible. Further, it is impossible to hold that the whole exists with absolute necessity, if there is any possibility of change in any part; therefore, the materialist must either deny that matter is necessary or he must reject the possibility of change. That there is change, however, is a fact of experience; new movements are produced in the universe. A consequence is that motion is not essential to matter; rather, matter receives motion from without; therefore, there is a God who gives this motion. Similarly, intelligence is not essential to matter, for rocks and wheat do not think. From what source, then, do sentient and thinking beings receive sensation and thought? This source cannot be themselves, for they sense despite themselves; it cannot be matter in general, for sensation and thought are not of its essence. Therefore, sentient and thinking beings have received these gifts of sentiency and intelligence from a supreme being who is intelligent, infinite, and the originating cause of all beings.[5]

There are, nonetheless, a number of objections, albeit specious ones, which can be brought against the two foregoing simple arguments proving God's existence. If God is not this material world itself, the objector argues, then God has created the world; but this would entail his having drawn it out of his own substance or his having drawn it from nonbeing. God cannot have drawn the material world from his own substance, for then it would be part of the divine essence; on the other hand, he cannot have made it from nothing, for from nothing, nothing comes. Further, if God made the world, he would have had to make it either freely or necessarily. If the latter, he would have had to be making it always, for his necessity is eternal and so the world would be eternal. What is eternal, however, cannot be created; these are contradictories. If one says, then, that God made the world freely, by pure choice, without any antecedent reason, an-

---

[5] *Ibid.*, p. 195. Despite Voltaire's scorn for the scholastics, he has reproduced here a species of collage of the Thomistic *secunda, tertia,* and *quarta viae* for proving God's existence. Moreover, in the succeeding part of the argument the author has even imitated the scholastic form of objections and answers to the objections. The immediate source of Voltaire's arguments, however, is more likely Locke's *Essay Concerning Human Understanding,* IV, x, 3–5 (Fraser edition, II, 307–09).

other contradiction ensues, for it is impossible to conceive of an infinitely wise being performing an action without any reason. Nor is it any easier to imagine an infinitely powerful Being spending an eternity without making the least use of his infinite power.

If these objections are not sufficient, there are still others. Though it seems to the generality of men that God has set the seal of his wisdom on all nature and that each thing in nature seems to be made for a certain purpose, to the eye of the philosophers it is even more evident that everything is accomplished in nature by the eternal, independent, immutable laws of mathematics. The construction and the durability of the human body are a consequence of the balance of fluids and the force of the various levers of which it is composed. The more discoveries that are made concerning the structure of the universe, the more evident it becomes that the whole fabric has been arranged according to mathematical laws. Therefore, it is reasonable to think that these laws, operating by their very nature, have produced the necessary effects which are mistaken as evidence of some arbitrary determination of an intelligent and powerful being. It is more reasonable, therefore, to say that a field produces grass because it is the nature of earth when watered by rain, than to say that grass grows because horses need it for their nourishment.

Furthermore, if the arrangement of the parts of this world and all that takes place among its sentient and thinking beings were produced by a creator and a master, one could only conclude that this creator was as barbarous as powerful. That is, if one admits final causes, then one will be obliged to say that the infinitely wise and infinitely good God has given life to his creatures only that they may devour one another; for a consideration of the animals found in the world leads to the conviction that each species has an irresistible instinct to destroy some other species. As for the evils which man suffers, they are such as to make it impossible for one to believe that God is just, unless one is to understand justice in a sense altogether different from the only meaning the word has when used in reference to men. Moreover, if the objection is made that justice as found in God is an entirely different justice, then it must be said that God is responsible for the ideas that man has and so is a deceiver, if he causes man to have an idea of justice which is altogether false. Whether one accepts the existence of God or inclines to atheism, there are absurdities to be swallowed, but surely it is easier to conceive of this visible world as eternal and infinite than to imagine an infinite and eternal being which we have never seen, and then to add creation to this explanation when no one has the slightest idea of what creation might be.[6]

All the foregoing objections, Voltaire says, can be reduced to the statement that it is impossible for us to conceive the manner of creation. This, however, is something quite different from proving that creation itself is impossible; one cannot argue from the impossibility of our thinking a thing to the impossibility of that thing's reality.[7] In order to prove the impossibility of creation itself, it would be necessary to prove that there is no God. Not only can one not prove such a thing, but one must admit that God exists necessarily, that it is impossible that he should not exist. The obscurity which accompanies the intellectual light by which we are aware of the existence of God is itself evidence of the validity of that light, for when we prove that God is infinite, we also prove that it is impossible that a finite being such as ourselves should comprehend this infinite cause. It seems, says Voltaire, that one composes only sophisms and speaks only absurdities when one attempts to deny the necessity of a self-existent being or to identify that being with matter.[8]

As for the argument that God could not have created the universe either freely or necessarily, it is sophistical; what it really states is only that the impossibility of one's understanding why

---

[6] *Traité*, Moland, XXII, 196–97. Voltaire seemed never to have too clear a notion of what he meant by creation; at least, it has proved impossible to find a definition of the term anywhere in his writings. However, from the contexts in which the term is used and from Voltaire's theory on the immutability of the elements, it would seem that creation means the bestowing on matter of a form which causes the matter to be a definite kind of thing. This is quite clear where there is question only of minerals; when there is question of plants, animals, and men, creation seems to be the ordering of minerals into a composite on which are bestowed the appropriate gifts of life, sensation, and thought. The minerals which are formed by creation and which make up living composites are absolutely immutable. The composites, however, may, and do, lose their gifts of life, sensation, and thought, but the constituent elements are unaffected by such loss. It is in the power of men to arrange pre-existing things, to put them together, to take them apart, to weigh and measure them; but only God can create. See *Histoire de Jenni, ou L'Athée et le Sage* (1775), Moland, XXI, 556.

[7] Voltaire himself uses this same argument, however, in denying the reality of an immaterial soul. He cannot imagine an immaterial soul; therefore, there is none.

[8] *Traité*, Moland, XXII, 197–98.

God would have created the universe at one time rather than at another entails the impossibility of God's having created it. This is like saying that one's inability to understand why a certain man did not exist a thousand years ago entails the impossibility of that man's existence at any time. Moreover, the free will of God is a sufficient reason to justify his choosing one time rather than another for the creation of the universe. If God exists, he is free; but to posit outside God a sufficient reason for his choice is to deny that he is free. On the other hand, to posit within God himself a sufficient reason is only to say that his will is his reason.[9]

Voltaire attempts to show that the argument that the universe operates according to immutable and eternal mathematical laws, and so is not created, is no less sophistical. These laws are not necessary in the sense that there could have been no other laws in the universe; the earth might have been placed differently from the way it now is. Moreover, these mathematical laws do not act by themselves; nothing acts without motion, and motion does not exist by itself. It is necessary, in order to explain motion, to have recourse to a first mover. Granted that the planets must pursue their present orbits in view of their quantity and their position in relation to the sun, it does not follow that they must have been given such a quantity, however, or been placed in such a relation to the sun. It is not even necessary that there be a certain number of planets, or of beings in general, as we can easily see from the daily changes in the number of beings. Therefore, from the farthest star to the least blade of grass, everything in the universe points to a first mover on whom depends the operation of the mathematical laws of the universe.[10]

In answer to the objection that not everything in the universe has a purpose, Voltaire replies that all we know with certitude is that we do not know the final cause of every being in the universe. When one sees a certain being, composed of an immense number of organic parts, producing a unique effect and always producing that effect, then only the person who has an inner re-

---

[9] *Ibid.*, p. 199. This position is contradictory to Voltaire's later argument that the universe must be eternal, because there must be an eternal cause of God's creative activity and that cause cannot be merely a capricious will.

[10] *Ibid.*, pp. 199–200. In later years Voltaire denies that anything could possibly be different from the way it actually is; but this is only after he had reached his final deterministic position.

luctance to admit the obvious conclusion can doubt that here is a
final cause. There is no more possibility, of course, of giving a
strictly demonstrative proof that the purpose of the stomach is to
digest food than there is for proving that it is day rather than
night. Still, the materialists will have even greater difficulty proving that digestion is *not* the purpose of the stomach.[11]

Finally, one who charges God with injustice and cruelty presupposes in his charge that there is such a thing as justice or morality. Neither of these, however, has a place in a system of materialism. It must be said that the ideas of justice which men have
are ideas that have been formed in them by society; justice among
men is always a matter of a relationship between one man and another. Justice, then, can have no application to God, and it is every bit as absurd to say of God that he is just or unjust in this
sense as it is to say that he is blue or square. Moreover, in order
to assert reasonably that it is cruel or unjust of God to permit men
and other animals to destroy one another, to countenance ill-
nesses and malevolent passions in men, to ordain that human life
should have a temporal limit, it would be necessary that one who
makes the assertion understand clearly that men and other animals *ought* to have the correlative perfections, that such perfections are *due* their nature. One can justly judge that a watch is defective only if one understands exactly what a watch is supposed
to do.[12] No one has such a perspicacious understanding of the
things of this universe that he would be justified in maintaining
that its limitations are evidence of a defect in the divine wisdom
or goodness.[13]

Some few years after having expounded the above arguments
in the *Treatise on Metaphysics*, Voltaire re-examined the same
problem in the *Elements of Sir Isaac Newton's Philosophy*. All
of Newton's philosophy,[14] we are told, leads inexorably to a
knowledge of the supreme being who has created all that there is

---

[11] *Ibid.*, p. 200.

[12] It is unfortunate that Voltaire did not use the consequences of this principle in the area of ethics. His confusion in ethical theory is due largely to
his inability to decide the question of man's final end.

[13] *Ibid.*, pp. 200–01.

[14] "Philosophy" here is obviously meant to include any kind of scientific
work, whether philosophy, taken strictly, or physics. The term, "philosophy," is used in this broad sense in the titles of works written by two of
Newton's friends and disciples: Colin Maclaurin's *An Account of Sir Isaac
Newton's Philosophical Discoveries* (London, 1775) and Henry Pember-
ton's *A View of Sir Isaac Newton's Philosophy* (London, 1728).

and has freely ordered everything. If, as Newton has shown, the world is finite and there is a void, matter cannot be a necessarily existing thing, and so it must have received its existence from a free cause. Matter has a gravitational force, but its gravity is not the very nature of matter, as is its extension; therefore, it must have received its gravitational force from God. If the planets turn in one direction rather than another in a nonresisting space, this is due to the absolutely free causality of their creator.[15] Still, for Newton, the strongest proof of the existence of God was the one from final causality. The infinitely varied designs in the greatest and smallest parts of the universe, though they lie within the reach of the senses and are therefore scorned by many philosophers, he regarded as being nothing other than the work of an infinitely skilled artisan.[16] Yet, the argument that an eternal and independent world is impossible because it would have as a consequence a succession of generations or effects, with neither an intrinsic nor an extrinsic cause, did not appeal especially to him.[17]

---

[15] *Eléments*, Moland, XXII, 404. Here Voltaire utilizes a few lines to deliver himself of the usual philippic against Descartes: the "pretended physical principles" of Descartes have served only to lead men's minds away from God and toward a dangerous precipice. The Cartesian system has produced that of Spinoza; many persons have been led by Descartes to admit no God other than the immense extent of material things. On the other hand, Voltaire has never met a Newtonian who was not a theist in the strictest sense. Voltaire's conviction that Spinoza was an atheist may very well be attributed to the *Dictionary* of Pierre Bayle, whose estimation of Spinoza was the popular one until Spinoza's own writings became better known and more widely read late in the eighteenth century. Bayle writes, in his article on Spinoza, "It is said, he died fully persuaded of his Atheism, and that he took some precautions to conceal his inconstancy, if there should be occasion for it. . . . Few people are suspected of adhering to his doctrine; and among those, who are suspected of it, few have studied it; and among the latter, few have understood it, and most of them are discouraged by the difficulties and impenetrable abstractions that attend it. . . . But of all Atheistical systems, none is less capable of deceiving than that of Spinoza; for, as I have said before, it is contrary to the most distinct notions of our minds." *Selections from Bayle's Dictionary*, edited by E. A. Beller and M. duP. Lee, Jr. (Princeton: Princeton University Press, 1952), pp. 307–09.

[16] *Eléments*, Moland, XXII, 414.

[17] It is possible that Voltaire knows this as a result of Newton's having criticized the type of proof that Voltaire had previously used. The objection Newton had to the argument that there must be some uncaused cause of any series of effects was that atheists who deny there is a void hold that there is, strictly speaking, no generation at all, for no new beings are produced; the universe is one whole, immutable in substance, existing necessarily, developing itself unceasingly, and infinitely varied in its modes. Consequently, an argument which proceeds from the assumption of a multiplicity of beings will not be conclusive. See *Eléments*, Moland, XXII, 405.

And this is justly so, says Voltaire, for there is scarcely a more striking proof or one which is more persuasive for man than the admirable order which reigns in the material universe.

When one observes the order which is found in the internal organs of an animal and the evident design in the varied manners of animal generation, nourishment, and growth, one recognizes without any difficulty that there is a sovereign artisan such as Newton sees at work in the universe. The fact that wolves eat lambs and spiders trap flies should not make one pause in giving assent; these continual generations and destructions are all part of the plan of the universe. If one would not call a farmer cruel because he raises animals that he might eat them, why should the artisan of the universe be termed rapacious if he causes animals to exist and to be eaten at their proper time? As for man, if he can have an eternity of happiness in another life, are the sorrows of this short life even worth mentioning? [18]

In the same work, *The Elements of Newton's Philosophy*, Voltaire comes to the defense of the great physicist against the attacks of Leibniz. The latter had objected that Newton's universe, with its diminishing motion, its increasing irregularities of the planets, and its bent toward dissolution unless put back to rights periodically by its author, had made God out to be a very poor workman, an artisan who had been able only to turn out a machine which required periodic adjustments. Therefore, Newton could not validly appeal to the order in the universe to prove there is a supremely intelligent being. Leibniz' difficulty, says Voltaire, is that he would like to have a *perfect* universe; but if man, the work of God's wisdom, is to perish, why should one not expect the world also to come to an end? Rather, if God formed the universe to endure for a certain time, then its perfection consists in lasting only until that moment fixed by God for its dissolution. Consequently, Leibniz is not able to show that Newton's physical theories, with their acknowledgement of imperfections in the universe, are inimical to the proofs for the existence of God.[19]

---

[18] *Eléments*, Moland, XXII, 407. This is just one more case in which Voltaire uses in one place a proposition which he attempts to disprove in another; Voltaire was never a champion of a doctrine of "an eternity of happiness in another life."

[19] *Ibid.*, pp. 418–19. The assumption here is that man is superior to the inanimate universe, but elsewhere Voltaire has argued that the sun is immensely more important than man, for the world can do very nicely with-

Though Voltaire himself occasionally had recourse to a "proof from motion," he came to regard such an argument as dubious, or at least not nearly so cogent as the proof from order in the universe. In the context of his exposition of the proof from design,[20] he advances some difficulties involved in arguing from the contingency and mutability of motion in the universe. If one attempts to convince the atheist by telling him that matter does not have motion of itself, for such motion would be essential to matter, and matter would then never be at rest, the atheist can object that rest is a mere fiction, an idea incompatible with the nature of the universe, that there is a constant quantity of motive force in the universe, that motion is therefore essential. Against these attacks, Voltaire says, the theist must take up still other weapons, though truth to tell, he himself does not know what they are. For this reason, Voltaire cannot help but regard the proof from design as the one which is the most striking. The verse, *Coeli enarrant gloriam Dei*, is, in his eyes, the finest argument ever offered, and it is with this verse that Newton fittingly closes his *Principles* and *Optics*.

Some years after completing the *Treatise on Metaphysics* and the *Elements of Newton's Philosophy*, Voltaire turned once again to the problem of the existence of God, and reiterated, in a dialogue between a philosopher and Nature, his opinion that the universe is a work of art. There is, he says, infinite art in the seas and mountains, in the structure of the tiniest insect, and in the order with which the rivers gravitate toward the center of the earth and are raised to the surface again. The philosopher is impelled to confess to Nature that she is the art of some great being, infinitely powerful and skillful, a being who conceals himself and manifests only his works. Still, the philosopher inquires, would it not be better that there should be nothing at all than that a multitude of beings should be formed only to be destroyed, that there should be sentient beings which experience so much pain and rational beings who rarely listen to reason? To this, Nature can only answer that the philosopher must inquire of the being who made her.[21]

---

out any given man, but without the sun, man and all living things would perish. For what is probably the source of Voltaire's defense of Newton against Leibniz, see *The Clarke-Leibniz Correspondence*, edited by H. G. Alexander, *passim*.

[20] *Eléments*, Moland, XXII, 405.

[21] "Nature, Dialogue entre le Philosophe et la Nature" (1771), *Q.E., Dialogues et Anecdotes*, Naves, p. 369.

In the *Questions on the Encyclopedia,* there appears again the argument from design, this time in answer to Holbach's *Système de la Nature,* and without the note of certitude which seems attached to the previously cited arguments. In this place, Voltaire states that the principal object of metaphysics is not to present arguments, but to consider whether, for the common good of the miserable thinking animals which are men, it ought to be admitted that there is a God who rewards and punishes. We argue in metaphysics, he says, scarcely otherwise than from probabilities; we are as people swimming in a sea whose shores they have never seen. However, those who are swimming with us cannot prove that there are no shores.[22] In fact, Cicero, Newton, and a not inconsiderable number of wise men have regarded the course of the stars and the structure of animals and vegetables as requiring that one admit the existence of a powerful hand which performs these marvels. And not only a powerful hand, but an intelligence also; for it is absurd to think that something which does not itself have intelligence should be able to bestow it on another.[23] If Holbach objects that we cannot tell where God dwells and so ought not admit His existence, then Holbach is being unphilosophical, for the fact that we cannot locate a cause in space is not a sufficient warrant for our denying that there is a cause.

Moreover, even the objection that men have sullied this universe with countless crimes, that men are wretched, is not valid. If one were to see a building constructed with consummate art, but stained with one's own blood and sullied by one's own crimes, one could not reasonably deny, in virtue of the building's disfigurement, that there was an architect. One who dwells in such a house, Voltaire continues, need not ask whether the architect is good or whether it would be better to leave than to stay, or whether the other inhabitants are satisfied with the house; all one needs to do to prove that God exists is ask whether such a con-

---

[22] "De la nécessité de croire un être suprême," *Q.E.,* Naves, pp. 518–19. In a letter to Crown Prince Frederick of Prussia, c. April 25, 1737, Voltaire had written: "All metaphysics that suits my taste contains two things: the first, what all men of good sense know; the second, what they will never know. We know, for example, what a simple idea is, and what a composite idea is, but we shall never know what it is that has these ideas. We measure bodies, but we shall never know what matter is. We can judge all these things only by way of analogy, a cane which nature has given to the blind. . . ." *Correspondence,* Besterman, VI, 126.

[23] "Dieu," *Q.E.,* Naves, p. 517.

struction, with all its beautiful apartments and wretched garrets, could have built itself.[24]

In the same work, *Questions on the Encyclopedia*, Voltaire repeats once more the argument that matter could not have produced intelligence, and that which produced it must itself be intelligent. When one sees a fine machine, one says that there is a good mechanic with a fine understanding of machinery. The world, similarly, is assuredly an admirable machine; therefore, there is in the world, wherever he might be, an admirable intelligence. Ancient though the reasoning may be, it is no worse for that fact. When we observe that all the living bodies in the universe are made up of levers and pulleys which act according to mechanical laws, of liquids which obey the laws of hydrostatics, that the stars and the planets move according to the most profound mathematical laws, it is impossible to contest the truth that there is an intelligent author of all this order.[25]

Those who cling to atheism argue, however, that motion alone has formed all that we see and all that we are. The present combination of particles of matter in the universe, they say, is possible; therefore, in an infinite duration, it necessarily comes to be. If one considers only four planets, Mars, Venus, Mercury, and Earth, one will see that there are only twenty-four possible arrangements of these planets in relation to one another. If one adds Jupiter, the chance that the planets would have their present arrangement is one in a hundred twenty; with Saturn, the possibility is one in seven hundred twenty. Adding the other planets, the stars, all vegetative, sentient, and rational beings simply increases the number of possibilities; and the possibilities are "infinite" only in the sense that we cannot comprehend the number. No matter how large the number of possibilities, one of them is the present arrangement of matter in the universe. And, given the eternity of matter, the present arrangement, not only *could*, but *must* at some time occur.[26]

To this argument Voltaire answers that the entire supposition of the atheists appears to him prodigiously chimerical, for two reasons. The first is that no one can prove that mere matter in motion could produce understanding. The second reason is that the atheist has himself admitted that there is only one chance in an in-

---

[24] *Ibid.*, p. 518.
[25] "Athée, Athéisme" (1770), *Q.E.*, Naves, pp. 459–60.
[26] *Ibid.*, pp. 460–61.

finite number that the world could have been formed without an intelligent cause, and when *one* is placed beside the *infinite*, one is a very small number indeed.[27] It is ridiculous to think that a blind force could cause the square of the revolutions of one planet to be always to the square of the revolutions of the other planet as the cube of its distance is to the cube of the distance of the others from a common center. Either the celestial bodies are themselves great geometers or there is an eternal geometer who has arranged them.[28]

If the modern atheist is still not content, but argues further that the various parts of animals are arranged in their present order because chance arrangements which were conducive to the conservation and propagation of the species have been perpetuated, while useless arrangements have perished, then it is for the atheist to explain how chance combinations of matter could produce sensation and understanding. Doubtlessly the various parts of animals are conducive to the well-being and propagation of the species, but this is because God has so designed them. A single wing of a fly is sufficient to overthrow atheism.[29] Nor does Maupertuis disprove the theistic position when he asserts that snakes, though they may be constructed beautifully, are good for nothing, that we ought not to admire an animal which we know only through the harm it does. By way of answer, Voltaire observes that, if flies could reason, they might very well complain to God of the existence of spiders, but they would avow, as Minerva did to Arachne, that they spin a wondrous web. It is absolutely necessary to admit an ineffable intelligence, whether it manifests itself in the stars or in the most vile creature. As for the evil which is found in snakes and other beings, we can only rejoice in the good and adore the eternal being who has produced the good and permitted the evil.[30]

In an article contributed to the *Encyclopedia* under the title, "God, Gods," Voltaire ties together in a few short sentences some of his arguments for the existence of a divine being. Among the few certainties which we have is the certainty that something

---

[27] *Ibid.*, p. 461.

[28] *Ibid.*

[29] *Ibid.*, pp. 461–62.

[30] *Ibid.*, p. 463. Pierre Moreau de Maupertuis (1698–1759), was a French mathematician and astronomer. For an account of the childish contest between Voltaire and Maupertuis for the favor of Frederick the Great, see Noyes, *Voltaire*, pp. 380–406.

exists. Because it is impossible that something should ever have come from nothing, the present existence of anything entails the eternal existence of something. We know also that a work which gives evidence of means ordered to an end is a sign of a workman; the universe, with its forces ordered toward its proper functioning, is such a work. There is, then, a mighty, most intelligent workman. This is a probability approaching the utmost certainty. One cannot deny the existence of the workman, but reason is unable to prove that the workman *made* the matter of which he formed the universe. All one can assert reasonably is that God is eternal and self-existent, that God and matter exist by the very nature of things. The explanation, however, of how *two* necessary beings should exist is not within the capability of human powers.[31]

Although Voltaire's later works make use of the argument from design as the most evident and most convincing of the demonstrations of God's existence, the *philosophe* returned occasionally, though with a decreased emphasis, to the argument from motion. In 1756 [32] and again in 1772 [33] he repeated the reasoning of the *Elements of Newton's Philosophy*. Motion is not of the essence of matter and must, therefore, be received by matter. That from which motion is received, however, cannot be another material thing, for that second material thing would have to receive motion from a third, and so on, *ad infinitum*. Therefore, there must be some immaterial being which produces motion in nature.

That Voltaire regarded the above arguments for the existence of God as capable of giving *certain* knowledge is a position somewhat difficult to maintain, but at least as difficult to disprove. We have already seen one passage in which Voltaire seems to hold that metaphysical arguments yield only probability, that accepting or rejecting the existence of God is to some extent a question of the utility, in terms of human happiness, of one or the other side of the question.[34] However, other passages, in which Voltaire expresses no such doubt about his reasoning, tend to indi-

---

[31] "Dieu, Dieux," *D.P.*, Moland, XVIII, 357. (Beuchot estimates that this article was written between 1765 and 1770.)

[32] *Dialogues entre Lecrèce et Posidonius* (1756), Moland, XXIV, 57–63.

[33] *Il faut prendre un parti* (1772), Moland, XXVIII, 520. The argument as originally stated can be found in *Eléments*, Moland, XXII, 434–35.

[34] "Dieu," *Q.E.*, Naves, p. 518. As was pointed out in the preceding chapter of this study, Voltaire did regard a conviction of God's existence as a prerequisite for personal and public morality for all except true philosophers.

cate that it might be wiser to interpret the former passage as implying two things: first, that the principal *purpose* of metaphysical speculation is not to argue or convince, but to weigh and decide whether it is better to admit that there is a God who will reward and punish; secondly, that it is not possible to prove with *mathematical* certitude that God exists. With respect to the first implication, it may be noted that Voltaire does not say metaphysics cannot present a valid argument, but only that he considers the *principal* object and interest of metaphysics to be a decision concerning the value of admitting the existence of God.[35] Moreover, it is a question here of a God who will reward and punish, and in none of his arguments to prove the existence of God has Voltaire pretended to prove that the supreme being will reward the good deeds of men and punish the evil. As for the second implication, Voltaire did not generally hold that his proofs had the same sort of certitude as those of mathematics. Moreover, in the same passage in which the author speaks of the metaphysician as a swimmer in an immense sea of whose shores he knows nothing, he inserts a plea to "adore with me the design which is evident in all nature and consequently adore the author of this design, the primordial and final cause of all." [36] It does not appear, then, that this passage can be intended to throw doubt on all the various arguments to which Voltaire had recourse in his attempts to demonstrate that there is an eternal, infinite, powerful, and intelligent being. And it is impossible to understand how such an eminent scholar as Daniel Mornet should write: "Au fond de lui-même Voltaire à l'ordinaire, est sans doute athée." [37]

However, in his *Cambridge Notebook*, Voltaire wrote that

---

[35] *Ibid.* "Le grand objet, le grand intérêt, ce me semble, n'est pas d'argumenter en métaphysique, mais de peser s'il faut, pour le bien commun de nous autres animaux misérables et pensants, admettre un Dieu rémunérateur et vengeur, qui nous serve à la fois de frein et de consolation, ou rejeter cette idée en nous abandonnant à nos calamités sans espérance, et à nos crimes sans remords."

[36] *Ibid.*, p. 519. "Adorez avec moi le dessein qui se manifeste dans toute la nature, et par conséquent l'auteur de ce dessein, la cause primordiale et finale de tout."

[37] Daniel Mornet, *Les Origines intellectuelles de la Révolution française* (*1715–1787*), p. 86. Mornet adds, "Il lui paraît qu'on ne peut croire à la liberté et à l'immortalité sans se heurter à des difficultés insurmontables. Mais cet athéisme n'est pas une des certitudes qui s'imposent, et il faut écrire comme si l'on était déiste." One possible explanation of Mornet's view is that Mornet based his conclusion on the literary, rather than the philosophical, works of Voltaire.

"God cannot be proved, nor denied, by the mere force of our reason." But even such a clear statement as this is saved from being a flat denial of the possibility of proving God's existence, for the list of propositions of which it forms a part is headed, "Guesses." Other "guesses" are that we may perhaps have eight senses, that we are of the same genus as the beasts but of another species, and that water, exercise, and sobriety may cure all diseases.[38]

Moreover, Voltaire counterbalances his occasional extravagances in the direction of skepticism by equally extravagant statements about the certitude of the proofs for the existence of God. In his *Homélies*, written in 1765, he writes, "I exist; therefore, something has existed from all eternity. . . . This truth is as demonstrable as the most evident propositions of arithmetic and geometry. . . . We are intelligent; therefore, there is an eternal intelligence." [39] That is, the existence of an eternal intelligence, God, is as certainly demonstrated as is the proposition, "Two

[38] *Voltaire's Notebooks*, I, 67.

[39] "Sur l'Athéisme," *Homélies* (1765), Moland, XXVI, 316: "J'existe, donc quelque chose existe de toute éternité. Cette vérité est aussi démontrée que les propositions les plus claires de l'arithmétique et de la géométrie. . . . Nous sommes intelligents: donc il y a une intelligence éternelle." Voltaire's statement of the certitude of this argument may have been copied from Locke. In the latter's *Essay Concerning Human Understanding*, he had written that the certitude that there is an eternally existing, intelligent being is comparable to the certitude that the angles of a triangle are equal to two right angles, IV, x, 2–12 (Fraser, II, 307–16). The list of passages in which Voltaire offers arguments to prove the existence of God is a long one: *Remarques sur les Pensées de M. Pascal*, Moland, XXII, 33, 57; letter of c. April 25, 1737, to Crown Prince Frederick, *Correspondence*, Besterman, VI, 125–26; "Athée," *D.P.*, Moland, XVII, 455; "Dieu-Dieux," *D.P.*, Moland, XVIII, 357; "Dieu," *Q.E.*, Naves, pp. 516–17; "Fin, Causes finales," *Q.E.*, Naves, pp. 538–39; "Philosophie," *D.P.*, Moland, XX, 210; "Platon," *Nouveaux Mélanges*, Moland, XX, 230; "Puissance, Toute-Puissance," *Q.E.*, Moland, XX, 296; and many others. In the face of the numerous instances of such proofs in Voltaire's writings, it is impossible to see how Kathleen O'Flaherty, in her *Voltaire, Myth and Reality* (2nd ed., Cork: Cork University Press, 1945), p. 91, when referring to the passages in which Voltaire proclaims his theism, can write, "These passages, if they are seen in the proper setting of Voltaire's work, appear mere exceptions for they are rare and almost, one might say, accidental. Placed beside the multitude of insulting references to God, as He is worshipped by others and not by M. de Voltaire and his friends, they become insignificant and rather unimportant." The references to the existence of God are scarcely "rare" or "accidental"; however, it is true that God, as Voltaire thinks of him, is not the God of the Scriptures, the God who creates freely, not from the necessity of his nature, and who has a regard for every sparrow that falls to the ground, for every hair of every man's head.

times two is four." It would seem, then, that it is reasonable to choose an interpretation which represents a *via media* between Voltaire's occasional lapses into somewhat wild statements about the certitude or lack thereof that he attaches to his proofs. The arguments are neither so evident as mathematical demonstrations, nor so devoid of validity as to have no claim to be called demonstrations of any sort.

While Norman Torrey's exposition of Voltaire's theism does not attempt to explain away the very real proofs Voltaire had offered, it is, in the light of the *philosophe's* text, somewhat fanciful. Had Voltaire, Torrey says, followed his rational premises he would have agreed with Diderot in the latter's "more scientific" account of the physical universe, and would "have been satisfied that the limits of human understanding had been reached and would have agreed with Diderot that the existence of God could not be proved and that the hypothesis of his existence helped to solve no problems of any kind." He did not, however, allow his reason to be his guide; rather, Voltaire was "betrayed by his mystical sense to seek a rational proof of the necessity of God as first cause . . . . the mystery of the universe could be sensed only in moments of mystic exaltation." [40]

The evidence Torrey has to substantiate his thesis is the article written on "Religion" for the *Questions on the Encyclopedia* in 1771:

> Last night I was meditating. I was absorbed in the contemplation of nature; I admired the immensity, the scope, the harmony of the infinite spheres which the common people are not able to admire. I admired even more the intelligence which presides over these works. I said to myself, "One must be blind not to be impressed by this view; one would have to be insane not to adore him." [41]

Then Voltaire proceeds to relate a "vision" which he had, somewhat in the manner of a Dante led by Virgil to the nether world. The "vision" is obviously not to be understood as anything more than a fanciful manner of stating that formal religion is produc-

---

[40] Norman Torrey, *The Spirit of Voltaire*, pp. 282–83.

[41] "Religion" (1771), *Q.E.*, Naves, p. 608. "Je méditais cette nuit; j'étais absorbé dans la contemplation de la nature; j'admirais l'immensité, le cours, les rapports de ces globes infinis que le vulgaire ne sait pas admirer. J'admirais encore plus l'intelligence qui préside à ces vastes ressorts. Je me disais: 'Il faut être aveugle pour n'être pas ébloui de ce spectacle; il faut être fou pour ne pas l'adorer.' "

tive of many vices, while the natural religion which Voltaire himself professes is productive of only the most elevated and enlightened behavior. If mysticism is nothing other than a feeling of exaltation when faced with the order of the universe, then Voltaire was, on at least one occasion, doubtlessly a mystic. His mysticism, however, was not of a supernatural order, Torrey says, but an experience of a humanistic kind, an exercise of a "cosmic sense," by means of which "his inner consciousness was attuned to the mysterious forces of the universe." [42]

In short, Torrey seems, on the one hand, to discount Voltaire's rational arguments for the existence of God and, on the other, to exalt the *philosophe's* emotional experiences with their consequences for morality and human happiness. Torrey's surmise that Voltaire's philosophical deism was often merely a useful weapon with which to attack Christianity must be measured against the very numerous and positive proofs of God's existence which are provided in Voltaire's writings.[43]

The question, however, of whether Voltaire's proofs of God's existence are valid can legitimately be asked. His own acknowledgement of the difficulty of showing that motion is not essential to matter seems to have only one solution: Newton maintains that there is a constant loss of motion and force in the universe, but no loss of matter. However, even if the real distinction between matter and motion be granted, there is still a considerable gap between the starting point and the conclusion that there exists a powerful, infinite, intelligent, immaterial being who has given to the universe its motion. While in general outlines the argument seems to be akin to the Aristotelian proof of a first mover, there are lacking the refinements of the Aristotelian argument: the definition of motion in terms of potency and act, the demonstration that whatever moves is moved by something other than itself, and the attempt to show that there could not

---

[42] Torrey, *The Spirit of Voltaire*, pp. 254, 283.

[43] *Ibid.*, p. 232. Peter Gay, in his *Voltaire's Politics* (Princeton: Princeton University Press, 1959), notes that Voltaire has been "much misinterpreted" concerning his position on the existence of God: "'If God did not exist, one would have to invent him,' probably the most notorious line Voltaire ever wrote, is not a cynical injunction to rulers to invent a divine policeman for their ignorant subjects. Rather, it is part of a vehement diatribe against an atheist, written in the midst of Voltaire's dialogue with Holbach." P. 265. In a footnote on the same page Gay cites Harold J. Laski as an example of misinterpretation of this phrase, in his *The Rise of Liberalism* (New York: Harper, 1936), p. 214.

be an infinite series of essentially moved movers. Moreover, the Voltairian argument involves quite an extensive logical jump from the premise that matter, as it is known in Newton's physics, is not essentially in motion, to the conclusion that the source of motion must be immaterial. Moreover, the conclusion of Voltaire's argument seems not to involve any presently existing being, but only one which at one time did exist and did give to matter the motion which it now has; or, at best, one which existed the last time there was an addition of force or motion in the universe.

With respect to the "most evident" demonstration, the one which rests on the impossibility of seeing a watch without concluding to the existence of a watchmaker, Voltaire, when faced with the objections of materialists, was able only to claim that his argument involved such a high degree of probability that the odds were infinity (in the sense of a number beyond man's ability to comprehend) to one, and that when one is placed over against infinity, one is a very small number indeed. He was not able to eliminate the one lone possibility that the material particles of the universe might have arranged themselves, by chance, in the order in which they now are. He does, however, note that sentiency and thought are attributes which cannot be explained merely by positing a certain arrangement of matter; they transcend matter. Therefore, even though the materialists have one possibility that the strictly material world is the result of chance movements, they have no explanation to offer for the genesis of sensation and thought. However, because Voltaire began his own argument for the existence of God with an observation, not of sensation and thought, but of the orderly construction and movements of the universe, his rebuttal of the materialists' objections amounts in a sense only to saying, "If my argument from order is not convincing, then I will construct another argument, taking as its starting point the fact that there are beings which sense and think." Nevertheless, inasmuch as the particular materialistic position which Voltaire was considering (that of Holbach) involved a premise that there was nothing outside the *plenum* of matter, his rebuttal does not completely miss the point.

The argument from sensation and thought, however, is quite unsophisticated. It is, to some extent, another version of the argument that motion is not essential to matter and therefore must have been given to matter by some being existing outside the material universe. Sensation and thought are not essential to matter, nor can they be the result of the motion of matter; therefore, they are given to matter by some being outside matter. Moreover, this being, inasmuch as it is the cause of sensation and thought, must itself be capable of knowledge to a degree higher than that which it bestows on matter. If, as Descartes had maintained, there were nonmaterial beings whose *essence* it was to think, then Voltaire's argument could not be granted. And on the level of immaterial substances, Voltaire could not make use of anything like Newton's dictum that motion and force are constantly being lost in the universe and so are not essential to matter. There was no one to whose authority Voltaire could appeal to show that the quantity of sensation or thought in the universe was constantly diminishing.

The argument which Voltaire himself calls the most metaphysical is likewise not completely devoid of difficulties. It might be noted, as a curiosity, that the starting point of this demonstration is quite a Cartesian and Lockean one: I exist.[44] From here Voltaire arrives at the existence of a necessary being, one which exists by reason of itself, and therefore eternally. The metaphysical principle involved in the demonstration is the contention that a being which has not always existed must have received its existence from some other being.

There is a difficulty involved here, however. Voltaire has said in too many other places that he does not think God is the total cause of matter, as if God had brought it into *existence;* rather, God has only given to matter its "form." In fact, Voltaire has stated clearly that he is not capable of imagining anything which did not previously exist, coming into existence. God is not a creator, he says, but only an orderer of previously existing matter, which is itself as eternal, and therefore as necessary, as God. In short, Voltaire's argument lacks the metaphysical groundwork which should have been provided by a more careful consideration of form as distinct from existence, and of necessary being as distinct from eternally existing being. No doubt the subtleties of the Thomistic distinction between existence and essence, on which St. Thomas Aquinas' argument from efficient causality depends, would not have appealed to the nonmetaphysical mind

---

[44] In his *Essay Concerning Human Understanding,* IV, x, 2–6 (Fraser, II, 307–10), Locke, too, had begun his proof of the existence of God with his consciousness of his own existence as a perceiving being.

of Voltaire. It is quite obvious, from the latter's inability to conceive of an eternally existing creative God without an eternally existing creation, that Voltaire had not spent much more time and energy than the average sage of the Enlightenment in studying the medieval writers who had raised and considered the questions which vexed the eighteenth century. This, however, is scarcely surprising in an age which considered itself to have arrived at the apex of human intellectual endeavor, to have achieved a wisdom compared with which most previous thought was mere sterile complexity and scandalous vapidity.

However, whatever the nature of Voltaire's proofs for the existence of God, whatever their deficiency, whatever their degree of certitude, it remains evident that the sage of Cirey considered the existence of God a fact easily arrived at by anyone who would study the material universe seriously. Moreover, it is evident that, for Voltaire, neither the world of inanimate beings nor that of men is fully intelligible until considered in relation to its intelligent cause, God. This relation, however, cannot be completely understood unless there is an understanding, not only of the existence, but also of the nature of God. The penultimate problem, then, in a study of Voltaire's constructive deism, is the *nature* of the causative term in the relationship existing between God and the universe.

CHAPTER SEVEN

The Nature of God

THOUGH VOLTAIRE SEEMS not to be conscious of any serious intellectual limitations when there is question of proving the existence of God, arriving at conclusions about the nature and attributes of the divine being is another matter. In one of his earliest passages on the subject, Voltaire himself states that, though one can only by means of sophistries and absurdities deny the existence of a necessary, self-existing being, establishing and discussing the attributes of this being is *tout autre chose*.[1] Nonetheless, throughout his philosophical writings Voltaire reverted frequently to the problem of the divine attributes, and considered in some detail the intelligence, infinity, beneficence, power, prescience, freedom, and unicity of God.

Voltaire's position on the question of whether intelligence can validly be predicated of God was greatly influenced by Locke, Clarke, and Newton. The "masters of logic," Locke and Clarke, Voltaire writes, argue that God must be intelligent, for whatever has produced the things of this universe must have the perfections of the things produced. Otherwise, the effect would be more perfect than the cause; there would be in the effect a perfection which was caused by nothing. Since there are intelligent beings in the universe, God must be intelligent.[2]

However, as if in demonstration of his statement that philosophizing about the attributes of God is a very difficult business, Voltaire observes that the argument of Clarke and Locke might be turned back against the theist. That is, if the existence of intelligent beings in the universe is evidence that God is intelligent, the existence of material things in the universe should count as equally valid evidence that God is material. To avoid this difficulty, one may hold with Clarke that divisibility and shape, the

---

[1] *Traité*, Moland, XXII, 198.
[2] *Ibid.*, p. 199.

inseparable attributes of matter, and even matter itself, are not perfections, but negations or limitations. Or, if one is not inclined to deny positive reality to matter, one may maintain that a cause may communicate to an effect some perfection which is *not* in the cause, or that matter has no cause, but is itself eternal and uncaused. If none of these possibilities can be asserted, then, Voltaire says, one can at least point out that the existence of material beings no more proves that God is material than the existence of intelligent beings proves that he is intelligent. The *philosophe* himself is not inclined to accept Clarke's solution, the one which would make matter a mere imperfection; he is inclined, rather, to regard matter as every bit as much a perfection as is thought.[3]

If this is true, that matter is as much a perfection as thought, and if it is true that a cause must have the perfection contained in the beings effected, and if it be granted also that God with his way of existing in all space is not like matter as we know it, extended in space, divisible, with dimensions, then it follows that intelligence as it is in God is not like intelligence as it is in man. It is possible that God should have created matter and spirit without being either of them as we know them.[4] They have not been derived from him as attributes of his substance, as Spinoza teaches; rather, they have been created by him.[5] In short, to adopt some

---

[3] *Ibid.* However, he is not absolutely sure of the meaning of "perfection"; whether it should be a question of perfection from man's point of view or from the divine viewpoint. As was pointed out in Chapter II of this study, Voltaire later solved this problem of divine materiality by positing matter as eternal and uncaused.

[4] *Ibid.*, p. 199. As late as 1771 Voltaire has not yet made up his mind concerning the possibility that God is an extended being. In the *Lettres de Memmius à Cicéron*, Moland, XXVIII, 452, he argues: "Why would not God, who is in all nature, be extended? In what respect is extension repugnant to his essence? If the great, intelligent, and necessary being operates on extended beings, how could he act where he is not? And if he is in all places where he acts, how is he not extended? A being whose existence in every particle of the world I would have to deny, one part after the other, would not exist in any part. 'A simple and incomprehensible being' is a phrase devoid of meaning, one which makes God worthy neither of more respect nor of more love; neither more powerful nor more intelligent. It is rather to deny him than to define him."

[5] "Creation" is a word often used loosely by Voltaire, and its use here must be interpreted in the light of other passages in which Voltaire regards the absolute beginning of a thing's existence as untenable. "Creation" can only mean "forming" or "setting in motion" or "endowing with attributes." In this particular place, Voltaire comes very close to stating a theory of

scholastic terminology, we can know *that* God is, but not *what* he is.

Léon Bloch, in his *La Philosophie de Newton*, gives some indication of one of the influences at work in forming Voltaire's mind with respect to what can be known of God, in what sense God can be said to be intelligent. Newton, Bloch says, held that it was praiseworthy to speak of God as hearing, seeing, speaking, rejoicing, loving, hating, accepting, giving, etc., because whatever we can say about God we say by way of comparison with what we have experienced. Though these comparisons are quite imperfect, they give us some faint idea of God. Still, one can never hope to *comprehend* the divine substance in this manner. Consequently, Newton would have held it to be correct to speak of God as intelligent; yet, this means only that there is some comparison possible between God and man with respect to knowing. Bloch points out that, while the philosophical approach of Newton and Voltaire is similar, while both admit that "intelligent" is neither a univocal nor an equivocal term when predicated of God, there is also a difference. Newton's philosophical "agnosticism" was compensated for by a supernatural revelation which made it possible for man to know more of God than philosophy alone would teach him.[6] For Voltaire, there was no such compensation; the ultimate

---

analogous knowledge of God, a knowledge by eminence and negation: God is at least as perfect as his effects; he is not like his effects in their imperfections; that knowledge we do have cannot be stated univocally; it is a knowledge which can be attained only by making some sort of comparison between the cause-effect relation existing between the universe and its "creator." Just exactly what this latter relation is, however, is not so clear that it can be stated univocally; therefore, the term of the causal relationship cannot be known clearly either.

[6] Léon Bloch, *La Philosophie de Newton* (Paris: F. Alcan, 1908), pp. 617–18. It is highly questionable that Newton accepted a supernatural revelation in more than a metaphorical or symbolic sense, whenever that revelation did not coincide with Newton's philosophical conclusions. Bloch, however, argues that Newton did not bother about setting up a metaphysical foundation for his science, because his religious faith, with its metaphysical implications, sufficed. *Op. cit.*, pp. 490–96. Edwin A. Burtt, in his *The Metaphysical Foundations of Modern Physical Science* (rev. ed., London: Routledge & Kegan Paul, 1949), pp. 283–84, however, writes of Newton that "he was a pious, believing Christian in all that term then implied, as well as a master scientist. His Arianism was radical for the age, but it did not prevent his approaching the world of science under the necessity of seeing it cloaked by a divine glory and suffused with the religious significance that followed from the conviction that it had been created and ordered by the hands of the God who had been worshipped from his youth as Father of the Christian Saviour and infallible Author of the Christian Scriptures." Louis

result was Voltaire's position that no more can be known of God than that He is one, eternal, powerful, and intelligent. And of these attributes, the most evidently demonstrated is that of intelligence; God is primarily, for Voltaire, a geometrizing shaper of pre-existent matter.

The question of the divine intelligence is a "metaphysical" question for Voltaire; that is, it is one that requires for its solution knowledge that surpasses sensation, knowledge that later followers of Locke's empiricism were to declare impossible of attainment. For Voltaire, too, despite his fascination with metaphysical problems, there recurred frequently the thought that answers to metaphysical questions were impossible. In 1744, at a time at which he was much influenced by Newton, but had rejected his original enthusiasm over the more metaphysical Clarke, Voltaire wrote:

> The more I advanced the more I became convinced that metaphysical systems are for philosophers what romantic novels are for women. One after another, they are all the rage, and then end by being forgotten. A mathematical truth remains eternally, and metaphysical phantoms pass away as things seen in a state of delirium. When I was in England . . . I said to a very enlightened person in whose company I was, "Mr. Clarke is a much greater metaphysician than Mr. Newton." "That may be," he answered me coldly, "but you might as well say that one is better at playing with balloons than is the other." This reply made me stop and think. I have since then dared to puncture some of those metaphysical balloons and have found that nothing comes out of them but hot air.[7]

Trenchard More, in his *Isaac Newton, A Biography* (New York: Scribner's, 1934), pp. 622–23, writes of Newton's theism as follows: "The leaders of the Church of England, and such men as Locke and Newton, accepted the Scriptures as a divine revelation and remained professing churchmen; while they might question the authenticity of some passages, they withstood the attacks of the then obscure deists who denied the truth of miracles as being contrary to the invariability of natural law."

[7] *Courte Réponse aux longs discours d'un docteur allemand* (1744), Moland, XXIII, 194. "Plus que je vais en avant, plus que je suis confirmé dans l'idée que les systèmes de métaphysique sont pour les philosophes ce que les romans sont pour les femmes. Ils ont tous la vogue les uns après les autres, et finissent tous par être oubliés. Une vérité mathématique reste pour l'éternité, et les fantômes métaphysique passent comme les rêves de malades. Lorsque j'étais en Angleterre. . . . je dis à un membre très-éclairé de la société: 'M. Clarke est un bien plus grand métaphysicien que M. Newton.— Cela peut être, me répondit-il froidement; c'est comme si vous disiez que l'un joue mieux au ballon que l'autre.' Cette réponse me fit rentrer en moi-même. J'ai depuis osé percer quelques-uns de ces ballons de métaphysique, et j'ai vu qu'il n'en est sorti que du vent."

Nevertheless, in one of the inconsistencies which crop up fairly often in Voltaire, having "once and for all" rejected metaphysical speculation, he never quite left off striving to know something more of the divine attributes than his stand on metaphysics would permit; and each time he concluded with an admission that man is incapable of understanding the divine nature. Yet, as is perfectly clear in Voltaire's repeated uses of the proof of the existence of God which takes its point of departure in the order Newton had discovered in the universe, Voltaire could never bring himself to doubt that God could truthfully and meaningfully be called intelligent.

Almost thirty years after the account of his renunciation of metaphysics, Voltaire observes, in an article on "Infinity," that we can have no more *positive* notion of infinity in matters of physical or moral power than we can have when there is question of the infinite divisibility, extent, and duration of matter. When we speak of the infinite power or justice of God, then we are only denying that we know any limit to his power or justice.

It is easy, Voltaire says, to perceive that a powerful, self-existent being has arranged the matter of the universe to form planets, metals, and animals, for these beings do not have the power to form themselves; but it is not so easy to understand the self-existent being's infinite power, justice, and goodness. Nor is it possible for us to understand the infinite extent of a being which is simple.[8] If we say of God's power that it is infinite, all we mean in reality is that it is very great. When we judge of his moral attributes, we necessarily judge according to our own conceptions derived from the picayune, uncertain, and variable justice and goodness we observe among ourselves. Thus, when we say that God is infinitely just or good, we mean only that his justice or goodness does not suffer from the limitations which accompany these virtues in the human beings of our acquaintance.[9]

That is, Voltaire's position on man's understanding of infinity agrees with that of John Locke. Infinity, in its primary meaning, is a "mode of quantity," a mere absence of a limit in our under-

---

[8] "Infini" (1771), *Q.E.,* Moland, XIX, 457–58. Voltaire is perhaps referring here to the Newtonian notion that God is in absolute space and, therefore, infinitely extended. How Voltaire arrived at the idea that God is simple, or, indeed, just what he means by "simple," is not evident from the context.

[9] *Ibid.*

standing of extension, number, or temporal duration. In a secon-ary sense, "infinite" can be applied figuratively to the power, wisdom, and goodness of God, inasmuch as man's understanding of them never exhausts their intelligibility and man's limited understanding can never fully comprehend them.[10]

Returning to his recurrent theme of the difficulty of understanding the divine nature, Voltaire observes that, when men insist upon pontificating about the divine attributes, it is not strange that we have one group assuring us that God has foreknowledge of all that will ever happen, though events are still contingent, and a second group assuring us that God is prescient in such a way as to exclude contingency from what is to come. There are even those who go so far as to maintain that, in the light of their knowledge of God's nature, they can state without fear of error that God can make a stick which has no ends and that he can make a thing to be and not to be at the same time. The consummate absurdity, however, has been achieved by Pascal, who thinks that he has explained the divine infinity by asking us to imagine a mathematical point moving everywhere with infinite swiftness: it is in every place and entire in each place. This, says Voltaire, is enough to make every sensible man tremble.[11]

Pascal, however, is not the principal enemy to be met, where there is question of the divine attributes; Pascal at least knows that God exists. Holbach and his *Système de la Nature* are another matter. Not only does Holbach fail to see that there must be some self-existent cause of the material universe, but he goes as far as to assert that what Voltaire regards as evidence of a beneficent God is really evidence that any such self-existent cause— though Holbach would not admit for a minute that any such exists—would be impotent and evil. Man, says the author of the

[10] John Locke, *Essay Concerning Human Understanding*, II, xvii, 1 (Fraser, I, 276–77).

[11] *Traité*, Moland, XXII, 199. Torrey makes an interesting observation about Voltaire's see-sawing between a denial, on the one hand, that man can know about God any more than that he exists, and, on the other, the repeated assertions about what can and cannot be truly said of God: "Concerning the attributes of God, Voltaire time and again expressed ignorance. It was impossible for him not to speculate, however. Deism was often merely a useful weapon with which to attack Christianity, and he was anxious, of course, to prove that the God of the deists was intelligent and good, while the Christian God was jealous and given to anger." *The Spirit of Voltaire*, p. 232. For Voltaire's general attack on Pascal, see J. R. Carré, *Reflexions sur l'anti-Pascal de Voltaire* (Paris: F. Alcan, 1935).

Système de la Nature, is the finest example of this impotency and malignity of his supposed creator, for man is a machine so fragile, so inconstant, so prone to disorders in its extraordinarily complicated mechanism that it would be preferable for him to be a stone. Then man would be incapable of feeling pain and distress of mind; he would be free from the manifold cares of life, incapable of suffering from remembrance of the past and anticipation of the future, immune from the dread of infinite torments in a future life.[12] Man, Holbach contends, is nothing other than a being formed by nature itself, by matter arranging itself without any transcendent geometrizing force. Indeed, if animalcules can be formed from mutton broth, as Holbach thought Needham had demonstrated, then men could just as well be formed from fortuitous chemical combinations.[13] This, in fact, we must hold if we do not wish to choose the alternative: a God who creates only to torture and destroy.

By way of answering those who find it impossible to admit the existence of a God other than one who is either impotent or cruel, Voltaire observes that man ought not ascribe to God attributes which are merely human. Man ought not make God in his own image and likeness. Human justice, human kindness, human wisdom are not predicable of God, even though we imagine these qualities with all limitations removed; one might just as well predicate of God infinite solidity, infinite motion, infinite roundness, or infinite divisibility. All the philosopher can say about God is that this universe must have been ordered by an incomprehensible, eternal, self-existing being; philosophy can give us no information concerning the attributes of this being: "We know what he is not, and not what he is." [14]

Where God is in question, there is no good or evil, either physical or moral. That is, since all the good and evil with which man is acquainted are inextricably bound up with human nature and are meaningless apart from it, they can have no applicability with

---

[12] "Fin, Causes finales" (1770), *Q.E.,* Naves, p. 540. See also Baron Paul Thiry d'Holbach, *Système de la Nature* (2 vols., London, 1781), II, 132–33. Pierre Naville, *Paul Thiry d'Holbach et la philosophie scientifique au XVIIIe siècle* (Paris: Gallimard, 1943), 109–15, has an interesting analysis of Voltaire's criticism of Holbach's *Système de la nature.*

[13] "Dieu," *Q.E.,* Naves, p. 517.

[14] "Nous savons ce qu'il n'est pas, et non ce qu'il est." "Bien," *D.P.,* Moland, XVII, 578. (Beuchot estimates that this article was written between 1765 and 1770. See Moland, XVII, viii–ix.)

respect to God. Nor can man reason, as Holbach attempts to do, that any first cause of man's nature and, therefore, of his sufferings, must be an evil being. Of all the evils which befall man, the worst is undoubtedly death. However, if man were to be immune from death, it would be necessary that man not be composed of parts, that he not be born, that he require neither the process of growth nor that of nourishment, that he should undergo no change. But such a being could scarcely be a man.

Moreover, if man were immortal, then other animals would be so also; and this would lead to an impossible situation; there would be a continuous reproduction of the various species until the earth would be so filled with them that there would be no means of sustenance for them. Death is not an error on the part of God; nor is it an evil or an injustice or a punishment.[15]

Something similar can be said for pain; in order that sentient beings be exempt from pain, all the laws of nature would have to be changed. That is, pain is a necessary consequence, in sentient beings, of the fact that matter is divisible, has weight, activity, and force. It is as contradictory to think that man should be free from all pain as it is to think that he ought not die.[16] Moreover, pain has its uses; were we never to experience pain, we would be perpetually injuring ourselves without being aware of the fact; it is only pain or a sensation of uneasiness which assures our performing the functions proper to life. Hunger stimulates man to take the food which is necessary for him; boredom moves him to work. Every desire is an incipient pain, and desire is requisite that man act at all. Pain is no more an error of Providence or an effect of malignity than is death.[17] All of this, as far as man's knowledge of God's attributes is concerned, adds up only to the thesis that, if a theist cannot demonstrate anything concerning the nature of God, much less can the atheist prove that God, if there were such, would be cruel and limited in power. Besides, "we are universally happy by our nature and unhappy only by accident. . . . Of a hundred thousand people there are not two who seriously desire to leave this life." [18]

---

[15] "Bien," *D.P.*, Moland, XVII, 578–79.
[16] *Ibid.*
[17] *Ibid.*
[18] *Extrait de la Bibliothèque raisonné* (1752), Moland, XXIII, 544. "Nous sommes donc universellement heureux par notre nature, et uniquement malheureux par accident. . . . Sur cent mille personnes, il n'y en a pas deux qui désirent sérieusement sortir de la vie."

In the *Il faut prendre un parti*, Voltaire states that those who proclaim that all is for the best are charlatans; nevertheless, whatever evil there is in the world is evil only in relation to man. In relation to God, "evil" has no meaning. A speaker representing the theistic position presents in this work what is Voltaire's own opinion on the subject:

> I shall assume that the good God, who has made everything, was not able to make it any better than he did. It is impossible that I should give offence to Him were I to say to him, "You have done all that a powerful, wise, and good being could have done. It is not your fault that your works could not be so good, so perfect as yourself. An essential difference between you and your creatures is the imperfection of the creatures. You could not have made gods. It was necessary that men, having reason, should also have some stupidity, just as all machines involve friction. . . . It seems to me impossible that an animal necessarily composed of desires and of acts of willing should not too often have the will to do himself a good turn by doing an evil one to his neighbor. It is only you who would never perform any evil act. Finally, there is necessarily such a great distance between you and your works that if goodness is in you, then evil must be in them." [19]

It is only by assuming that "good" and "evil" as they are used in reference to man can also be meaningfully predicated of God that men can argue that God must be cruel or impotent. Whenever man attempts to say more about God than that he is one, eternal, powerful, and intelligent, he attempts the impossible and falls into some absurdity. [20]

In another place Voltaire approaches the question of God's power. Does man have reason for thinking that the divine being is infinitely powerful? Has anyone the ability to understand in-

---

[19] *Il faut prendre un parti*, Moland, XXVIII, 548–49. "Je supposerai que le bon Ormase, qui a tout fait, n'a pu faire mieux. Il est imposssible que je l'offense quand je lui dis: Vous avez fait tout ce qu'un être puissant, sage et bon, pouvait faire. Ce n'est pas votre faute si vos ouvrages ne peuvent être aussi bons, aussi parfaits que vous-même. Une différence essentielle entre vous et vos créatures, c'est l'imperfection. Vous ne pouviez faire des dieux: il a fallu que les hommes ayant de la raison, eussent aussi de la folie, comme il a fallu des frottements dans toutes les machines. . . . Il me paraît impossible qu'un animal, composé nécessairement de désirs et de volontés, n'ait pas trop souvent la volonté de se faire du bien en faisant du mal à son prochain. Il n'y a que vous qui ne fassiez jamais du mal. Enfin il y a nécessairement une si grande distance entre vous et vos ouvrages que si le bien est dans vous, le mal doit être dans eux."

[20] *Ibid.*, p. 534.

finity at all, that he might have any notion of infinite power? What man *can* know is that there is a supreme intelligence powerful enough to form men, to preserve them for a limited time, to reward and punish them. This, it would seem, is not sufficient evidence to conclude that God can do more than this; reason cannot prove that a being is capable of doing more than it has actually done. There is no proof that God could make the life of animals longer, that he could form things without destroying others in the process; it is quite possible that God does only those things his nature compels him to do and that he can do no more. Indeed, this latter view seems to be most reasonable; for, if one says that God was able to form sentient beings in a state of eternal enjoyment, but did not, then one would have to say that he was lacking in goodness. However, one should not fear to look upon God as a power of very great extent, but still circumscribed within certain limits by his very nature.[21] Nor is this of any consequence to man; man is as much subject to a God of limited power as he would be to an infinitely powerful God.

Again, there is no detraction from the honor man owes to God, if man regards him as producing the creatures of the universe because he was determined by his nature to do so, rather than because it happened to be his will and good pleasure. At least, it is better to admit the existence of a limited God who determines all by his very nature than to leave to the atheist his argument that God is cruel or else nonexistent.[22] Nor is it strange to think that God is limited in power. There are certainly many things which the supreme intelligence could not prevent; for example, that the past should have been or that the future should follow the present. The list of these impossibilities would be very long. Is it not, therefore, quite reasonable to think that God was not able to prevent evil?[23]

Though one is compelled by the evidence to admit that there is an intelligence permeating the entire universe, one has no reason for asserting that this intelligence has a knowledge of the future. In fact, it is impossible to explain how a being could see what does not exist; to "foresee" is only to conjecture. Christians, who maintain that God was able to foresee that an enemy would destroy this world and still freely created it, have the problem of

---

[21] "Puissance-Toute puissance" (1771), *Q.E.*, Moland, XX, 298–99.
[22] *Ibid.*
[23] *Lettres de Memmius a Cicéron*, Moland, XXVIII, 450.

explaining how it is consonant with the dignity of God that he should be an accessory to his own perpetual defeat. Rather than assert that God is prescient, it is better to admit that whatever he does, he does necessarily. The more prudent position is that God, acting always for the best, has done the best he could do.[24] When one considers carefully the death of newborn infants, the lifelong misery of many persons, such scourges as smallpox, famine, the Inquisition, and the misfortune that human bladders should turn to stone quarries, then one can only grant that all is necessarily a consequence of the divine nature.[25]

Nevertheless, the necessity that one discovers in God, the fact that God acts as determined by his nature, does not require that one deny that God is free. In the *Il faut prendre un parti*, Voltaire writes:

> It is evident that this supreme, necessary, active intelligence has a will and that he has ordered everything because he has willed to do so. How could one act and bring order into things without willing to do so? To act in such a way would be to act as a mere machine, and such a machine would presuppose a prior principle, another mover. It would always be necessary to return to a first intelligent being, whatever he might be. We will, we act, we build machines when we will to do so; therefore, the great, very powerful demiurge has made everything because he willed to do so. . . . an intellect devoid of a will would be an absurd thing, for such an intellect . . . would not will to do anything. The great necessary being has, therefore, willed everything that he has effected. . . . But would not this necessity make his will useless? Doubtlessly not, for though I necessarily wish to be happy, I do not by reason of this necessity wish it any the less; on the contrary, the more irresistibly I wish for happiness, the more forcefully do I wish for it. Does this

---

[24] "Puissance-Toute puissance," *Q.E.*, Moland, XX, 299. In the *Essai sur les moeurs et l'esprit des nations* (1765), Moland, XI, 94, however, Voltaire writes: "If the eternal being, who has foreseen everything, who governs everything by immutable laws, should become opposed to his very self by upsetting all his laws, this could be only for the good of all nature [not, Voltaire means, for the advantage of but one particular human being]. But it would seem to be contradictory to suppose a case in which the creator and master of all things could change the order of the world for the good of that world. For, either he would have foreseen the pretended need there would be for such a change or else he would not have foreseen it. If he had foreseen it, he would have ordered things in accordance with that foresight from the very beginning; if he had not foreseen it, he would no longer be God."

[25] "Puissance-Toute puissance," *Q.E.*, Moland, XX, 299.

necessity in the great being take away his freedom? Not at all. Freedom can be nothing other than the power of acting. The supreme being, because he is very powerful, is therefore the most free of all beings.[26]

Nor does this freedom entail a denial of the proposition that everything which exists exists necessarily; "creation" is both free and necessary. If one maintains that God brings about effects without being determined by either his own nature or by anything outside himself, then one is simply maintaining that here is an example of an effect without a cause. Just as it is impossible for the world to exist without the eternally existing God, so is it impossible for God to exist without the eternally caused world.[27] The divine freedom consists only in the power of acting. God has acted eternally and fully; therefore, he has always used the fullness of his liberty.[28]

When Spinoza, on this question of the divine will, expresses the opinion that one can justly say neither that God has a will nor that he has the ability to order materials intelligently, Voltaire objects that men, who are but modes of the divine substance in Spinoza's system, have wills and the ability to design; therefore, the infinite, necessary, absolute being cannot be deprived of them.[29]

---

[26] *Il faut prendre un parti*, Moland, XXVIII, 523–24. "Il est clair que cette suprême intelligence nécessaire, agissante, a une volonté, et qu'elle a tout arrangé parce qu'elle l'a voulu. Car comment agir et former tout sans vouloir le former? Ce serait être une pure machine, et cette machine supposerait un autre premier principe, un autre moteur. Il en faudrait toujours revenir à un premier être intelligent, quel qu'il soit. Nous voulons, nous agissons, nous formons des machines quand nous le voulons: donc le grand Demiourgos très-puissant a tout fait parce qu'il l'a voulu. . . . une intelligence destituée de volonté serait une chose absurde, parce que cette intelligence. . . . ne voudrait rien opérer. Le grand Etre nécessaire a donc voulu tout ce qu'il a opéré. . . . Mais cette nécessité lui ôterait-elle sa volonté? Non, sans doute; je veux nécessairement être heureux, je n'en veux pas moins ce bonheur; au contraire, je le veux avec d'autant plus de force que je le veux invinciblement. Cette nécessité lui ôte-t-elle sa liberté? Point du tout. La liberté ne peut être que le pouvoir d'agir. L'Etre suprême, étant très-puissant, est donc le plus libre des êtres."

[27] "Philosophie" (1765), *Nouveaux Melanges*, Moland, XX, 210–11.

[28] *Ibid.* J. R. Carré gives in the articles, "Voltaire philosophe," *Revue des Cours et Conférences*, XXXIX (1938), 98–108, 193–211, 289–307, 531–52, 606–25, what is perhaps the best available exposition of Voltaire's constructive deism, but even Carré neglects the importance of Voltaire's theory that the activity of God in forming the universe is completely determined.

[29] "Dieu-Dieux" (1771), *Q.E.*, Moland, XVIII, 368. There is a vast difference between saying, as Voltaire does, that in Spinoza's system men are said to have wills, and saying, as Spinoza himself does, that men may, by having

Where there is question of saying anything further about the divine being, however, man can best practice prudence by practicing silence. If one asks where the eternal geometrician is, whether he is in one place or in all places without occupying space, whether he has made the universe of his own substance as Spinoza maintains, whether he is immense but without quantity and quality—to these questions the cautious man can answer only that he does not know.[30] With our feeble knowledge and limited intelligence we cannot answer such questions. We have no adequate idea of the divinity; we stumble along from one conjecture to another. In short, on the question of the divine attributes, Voltaire is too good a Lockean to admit anything like a clear knowledge of properties which have not been experienced by means of the senses, but he is also inclined on occasion to grope toward the notion that there is a kind of non-univocal knowledge of God which is based on positing a causal relationship between the non-sensible first cause and the universe accessible to the senses.

There is, however, one more proposition which can be asserted about the supreme being: he is unique; there is only one God. In his rather late work, *Tout en Dieu*, Voltaire argues that

> there is only one universal, eternal, and agent principle in nature. There could not be two, for they would be either alike or different. If they were different, they would destroy each other; if they were alike, they would be as one. The unity of design in the infinitely varied universe is evidence of a single principle.[31]

---

adequate ideas, be active causes of their desires. In the Appendix to the *Ethics*, Spinoza writes, "All of our endeavors or desires *so follow from the necessity of our nature*, that they can be understood either through it alone, as their proximate cause, or by virtue of our being a part of nature, which cannot be adequately conceived through itself without other individuals." Italics added. *Improvement of the Understanding, Ethics, and Correspondence* (translated by R. H. Elwes, London: M. W. Dunne, 1901), p. 242. Voltaire's apparent ignorance of Spinoza's doctrine of adequate ideas in relation to human causality may be due to the fact that Bayle did not include, in his article on Spinoza, any reference to this doctrine.

[30] "Athée, Athéisme" (1770), *Q.E.*, Naves, p. 461.

[31] *Tout en Dieu, commentaire sur Malebranche* (1769), Moland, XXVIII, 97. "Il n'y a dans la nature qu'un principe universel, éternel, et agissant; il ne peut en exister deux: car ils seraient semblables ou différents. S'il sont différents, ils se détruisent l'un l'autre; s'ils sont semblables, c'est comme s'il n'y en avait qu'un. L'unité de dessein dans le grand tout, infiniment varié, annonce un seul principe." While Pierre Bayle, in the article on the Manichees, had discussed the possibility of two ultimate principles in the uni-

This argument is interesting, not for its cogency, but for its clear statement of Voltaire's confidence that there is only one God. The argument that two *unlike* universal principles would destroy each other is perhaps based on an assumption that two such principles would be something like the Manichaean principles of good and evil and could not possibly cooperate or act in concert. That two *like* principles would be as one could be justified only by recourse to some such tenet as the Leibnizian theory of the identity of indiscernibles—which Voltaire might very well have accepted even though he would be loath to admit that he had learned it from Leibniz. The argument continues:

> If it [the universal principle] acts on all being, it acts on all the modes of all being; there is, therefore, not a single movement, a single mode, a single idea which is not the *immediate* effect of a universal, ever-present cause. . . . This cause has always acted. It is as impossible to think that a being, by his nature essentially acting, would have been idle a whole eternity as it is to think of a luminous being existing without light. A cause without an effect is as much a chimera, an absurdity, as an effect without a cause. Therefore, there have always been, and always will be, effects of this universal cause.[32]

Only monotheism, then, is a reasonable form of natural religion. True, Voltaire notes, there have been polytheistic religions

verse without giving any decisive arguments against such a possibility, he did, in one short passage, argue in a manner which might have suggested to Voltaire a proof for the unicity of God: "The most certain and most clear ideas of order we have, teach us, that a Being which exists by itself, which is necessary and eternal, must be one, infinite, almighty, and endowed with all kind of perfection. If therefore we consult these ideas, we shall find nothing more absurd, than the hypothesis of two eternal principles, independent of one another, one of which has no goodness, and can put a stop to the designs of the other." *Selections from Bayle's Dictionary*, p. 169.

[32] *Ibid.* Italics added. "S'il agit sur tout être, il agit sur tous les modes de tout être: il n'y a donc pas un seul mouvement, un seul mode, une seul idée, qui ne soit l'effet immédiat d'une cause universelle toujours présente. . . . Elle a donc agi toujours. Il est aussi impossible de concevoir que l'Etre éternel, essentiellement agissant par sa nature, eût été oisif une éternité entière qu'il est impossible de concevoir l'être lumineux sans lumière. Une cause sans effet est une chimère, une absurdité, aussi bien qu'un effet sans cause. Il a donc eu éternellement, et il y aura toujours des effets de cette cause universelle." That a principle which acts on all beings must, as a consequence, act on all modes of beings in such wise as to be their immediate cause is not proved by Voltaire; nor does it seem to be self-evident. The fact that Voltaire does not define "mode" lends additional obfuscation to the passage.

among primitive peoples, but this fact is due simply to their having arrived at a knowledge of God through the things of their experience; the wondrous occurrences in nature, harvests, storms,
and scourges of various kinds, revealed to them the hand of a
master.[33] Then leaders were necessary to rule in society, and it
was requisite that these rulers, to whom the people were accountable, should have over them other sovereigns to whom they
would be accountable in turn, and so each tiny society had its own
god. However, because each small state desired that its ruler
should be more powerful than the rulers of the neighboring states,
each group, making use of the natural ability to reason by
analogy, imagined that, although it was quite all right for the other
groups to have their own ruler and so their own god, the god of
its own tribe was superior to the gods of the neighboring tribes.
Nor has there ever been a polytheistic nation which did not regard
one of its gods as supreme and the sole architect of the universe.[34]
Moreover, the idea of a unique sovereign being exercising his
providence over the universe is found in the writings of all the
philosophers and poets; it is as unreasonable to think that the
classical writers regarded their heroes, genii, and inferior gods
as equal to the "father and ruler of the gods" as it would be to
think that Christians equate the blessed and the angels with God
himself.[35]

In 1772 Voltaire wrote what is perhaps a good, concise summary of his final position concerning what can be known of
the divine attributes. The principle of action must be unique. The
constant uniformity of the laws which direct the progress of the
celestial bodies, the uniformity of the motions of the earth, the
uniformity of each species and each genus of animal, vegetable,
and mineral is an indication that there is only one mover.[36]

> This unique mover is very powerful, for he directs such a vast
> and complex machine. He is very intelligent, for the least of the
> workings of this machine could not be matched by us, who are in-

---

[33] "Dieu-Dieux," *D.P.*, Moland, XVIII, 357.

[34] "Dieu," *Q.E.*, Naves, pp. 505–06. In the article, "Religion" (1765), *D.P.*,
Naves, p. 360, Voltaire gives an argument purporting to show that monotheism was the primitive form of religion and that polytheism was a cor-
ruption of the pristine purity of natural religion.

[35] "Polythéisme" (1761), *Mélanges, D.P.*, Moland, XX, 244.

[36] *Il faut prendre un parti*, Moland, XXVIII, 549. "Je me confirme dans
cette idée qu'il ne peut exister qu'un seul principe, un seul moteur, dès que
je fais attention aux lois constantes et uniformes de la nature entière."

telligent. He is a necessary being, for without him the machine would not have existed. . . .[37] "He is eternal," Voltaire continues, "for he could not have been produced from nothing, which, being nothing, can produce nothing. Because something now exists it can be demonstrated that some being has existed from all eternity."[38]

These attributes, then, unicity, power, intelligence, and eternity, are all that we can know about God. Beyond this, there are only questions and speculations.

Nevertheless, these attributes, as they are understood by Voltaire, determine the *philosophe's* position on the relationship existing between the world of nature and God. That is, it is on his tenuous understanding of the divine nature that Voltaire bases his constructive deism. And, even though an empirical study of the physical universe precedes, in the Voltairian methodology, any metaphysical speculation concerning the existence and nature of God, the *philosophe's* solutions to these metaphysical problems influence, in turn, his interpretation of the evidence offered by the empirical study. That is, not only does his study of nature determine his metaphysical position, but his metaphysical position also determines, to no small degree, his philosophy of nature. This becomes most clear in an analysis of the central problem of Voltaire's constructive deism: the relationship existing between God and the world of nature.

---

[37] The argument Voltaire uses here is a peculiar one: whatever is, is necessary, for all happens as a consequence of the divine nature. Now, because the universe is necessary, its cause is necessary. Therefore, God is a necessary being. The logical structure of this argument is at least open to question.

[38] *Ibid.,* p. 520. "Ce moteur unique est très-puissant, puisqu'il dirige une machine si vaste et si compliquée. Il est très-intelligent, puisque le moindre des ressorts de cette machine ne peut être égalé par nous, qui sommes intelligents. Il est un être nécessaire, puisque sans lui la machine n'existerait pas. Il est éternel: car il ne peut être produit du néant, que n'étant rien, ne peut rien produire, et dès qu'il existe quelque chose, il est démontré que quelque chose est de toute éternité."

CHAPTER EIGHT

The Relationship Existing between God and the World of Nature

ONCE VOLTAIRE HAS ARRIVED at the knowledge of God's existence and has attained some vague understanding of the divine nature, a complete picture of the Voltairian universe begins to emerge. While it is evident that God is the one cause of all that occurs in the world of nature, the details of the picture are missing until it is made clear that God is this unique cause through the mediation of universal laws, that these laws are absolutely unchangeable, and that the divine causality extends even to physical and moral evil. In order, then, to grasp as completely as possible Voltaire's constructive deism, his theory of the relationship existing between God and the world of nature, it is necessary to give careful consideration to these details of the picture.

In the *Treatise on Metaphysics* there is a quite definite statement of Voltaire's attitude on the relation of God to the universe he has created: God has put men and animals on earth, but it is up to them to get along there the best way they know how. Certainly it is unpleasant for the fly that falls into the spider's web and for the sheep that encounters a wolf; but if the sheep were to say to the wolf, "You are deficient in moral goodness," the wolf would answer that it was a question of the wolf's own physical welfare and that God does not seem to care too much whether the sheep is eaten or not. The best policy for the sheep, therefore, is to stay close to the shepherd. Nor do men fare much better. God has not handed down from heaven, Voltaire says, any set of moral laws for the individual or society; in fact, those who have pretended to impose God-given laws on man have not given even a ten-thousandth part of the rules necessary for the conduct of life. Although Voltaire does not say so, it would seem from the context that God has no more concern about one man's injustice to another than he has for the sheep eaten by the wolf.[1]

While one might expect that the *Poem on the Lisbon Disaster* would give some indication of the relation of God to the universe, some explanation reconciling the existence of an infinitely good and powerful God with the suffering and death of thousands of innocent persons, Voltaire has no solution to offer. In fact, in a note added in 1756 he says that the question of such an explanation is as likely to be solved as the proverbial problem, which came first, the chicken or the egg? [2] However, Voltaire's later writings yield ample evidence that his general position on the matter was that God, the eternal geometer, had informed matter according to certain general laws and then left it to its own devices. However, this general notion involves certain difficulties with respect to Newton's unquestioned "discovery" of a loss of force in the material world and an increasing deviation of the planets from their paths, entailing either a run-down and disordered universe in the future or some divine intervention to restore lost force and order. A further problem is the continuing inception of life in animals, something which Voltaire seems on occasion to regard as requiring some divine causality other than the initial ordering and moving of the universe. There is also, though the question has already been dealt with in Chapter IV of this study, the problem of explaining the manner in which God is a cause of man's specifically human actions.

Natural, physical, mathematical laws appear to be for Voltaire the link between God and the universe. There is, he says, an admirable mathematical principle guiding all of nature and effecting everything produced. That birds fly and that fish swim are effects of the known laws of motion. The sensations and ideas which men and animals have can scarcely be anything other than effects of more refined and less obvious laws. With the ideas caused by these more refined mathematical laws, animals are necessarily impelled to seek what is for their physical welfare. There is one mainspring, one mathematical order, which regulates the entire universe.[3] By reason of this one mainspring, God gives to

---

[1] *Traité*, Moland, XXII, 229.

[2] *Poème sur le désastre de Lisbonne* (1756), Moland, IX, 477.

[3] "Idée" (1771), *Q.E.*, Naves, p. 557. Voltaire often writes as if mathematical laws were subsistent in such wise that they might exercise an efficient causality on the universe, or as if they were at least a formal principle

men all they possess: their physical organs, their sensations, and the ideas which follow upon the sensations. Everything is an operation of God upon his creatures, an operation proceeding according to eternal, immutable, mathematical laws. While those who propound systems such as that of physical premotion would have God occupied with what goes on in the head of each individual Jansenist or Molinist, one who understands aright knows that the being of beings is concerned only with the great and general laws of the universe, the arrangement of the entire system of the universe.[4]

In the *Il faut prendre un parti*, which is perhaps the short work which best summarizes Voltaire's mature thought, there is an epitome of his doctrine of the complete subjection of the universe to universal laws:

> All these beings are equally subject to eternal and invariable laws. Neither the sun, nor the snail, nor the oyster, nor the dog, nor the monkey, nor men are able to give themselves what they possess; it is evident that they have received everything. . . . From whom do they receive their powers if not from the primordial, eternal cause, the principle of action, the great being who gives life to all nature? . . . It would be a strange contradiction, a singular absurdity, if all the stars, all the elements, all the vegetables, all the animals should obey unceasingly and irresistibly the laws of the great being while man alone should be able to determine his own path of action. . . . we are only blind instruments of nature. . . . The universal principle of action does everything in us. He has not at all excepted us from the laws governing the rest of nature.[5]

within the things of nature. However, he just as often, as happens in this passage, removes the impression by referring to God as the efficient cause acting *according* to mathematical laws. To what extent, if any, these laws are independent of God in the manner of Leibnizian essences or to what extent they are consequences of the divine nature is never quite clear enough to settle the issue beyond the possibility of a question.

[4] *Ibid.*, pp. 558–59.

[5] *Il faut prendre un parti*, Moland, XXVIII, 524–26. "Mais tous ces êtres sont également soumis aux lois éternelles et invariables. Ni le soleil, ni le colimaçon, ni l'huître, ni le chien, ni le singe, ni l'homme, n'ont pu se donner rien de ce qu'ils possèdent; il est évident qu'ils ont tout reçu. . . . De qui tiennent-ils toutes ces facultés, sinon de la cause primordiale éternelle, du principe d'action, du grand Etre qui anime toute la nature? Ce serait une étrange contradiction, une singulière absurdité, que tous les astres, tous les éléments, tous les végétaux, tous les animaux, obéissent sans relâche irresistiblement aux lois du grand Etre, et que l'homme seul pût se conduire par lui-même . . . . nous ne sommes que les instruments aveugles de la nature. . . . Le principe universel d'action fait tout en nous. Il ne nous a point exceptés du reste de la nature."

There are two constantly repeated experiences, Voltaire continues, which serve to convince him, and all men who seriously consider the matter, that man's ideas, his acts of willing, his actions are not his own. The first experience of our consciousness is that we do not have, and cannot have, any certain knowledge about what ideas we shall have, what choices we shall make, or what physical motions we shall perform in the very next moment. If we think and act without having previously known what we shall think and do, obviously we cannot be the cause of those thoughts or actions.

Before proceeding to the second "experience" Voltaire lists, it might be well to note that the first "experience" is liable to no slight degree of criticism. While it is true that many of the thoughts man has are in some sense a surprise to him, it is no less true that man in some cases deliberately directs his thoughts to a subject previously chosen. One can choose to concentrate on a mathematical problem, on a letter to be written, on a philosophical puzzle, or even on the writings of Voltaire. Evidently one does not have to begin with the elaborated thoughts that one has after deciding to concentrate, but it is contrary to experience to claim that all man's thoughts take him by surprise and lie completely beyond his control.

Voltaire, it would seem, is arguing from the premise that one cannot have a thought before he has it; and the premise seems sufficiently self-evident to satisfy even the most rigorous logician that it needs no proof, that it is a mere tautology. However, if one distinguishes—a process which never ceased to irritate Voltaire and his anti-scholastic prejudices—between thoughts which are the same numerically and those which are the same with respect to content, the premise becomes ambiguous. No one can have the numerically same thought twice, for if thoughts can be numbered at all, it is only by reason of the time at which one has them. That one can have two numerically distinct thoughts which are the same, however, with respect to content, is evident from experience. Certainly a geometer whose thought of "triangle" differed in content each time he entertained it, would constitute a walking absurdity. Contrary to Voltaire's claim, a geometer can choose to think of triangle precisely because he has previously thought of triangle and knows now exactly of what he wishes to think. Similarly, one can choose to relive in an imaginary manner some pleasant—or unpleasant—experience of the past; the choice is possible precisely because one has had the same thoughts in the past. This, of course, is not intended to deny that many, or most, or perhaps almost all the thoughts that come to a man during a day lie outside the field of his free choice.

As for one's not knowing what he will choose in the next moment, the very nature of choice requires that something be known as a possible object of choice, and there is no denying that we do have such knowledge. It is not the choice that is chosen, though one may, by a kind of reflexive process choose to choose; it is the object, whether it be a thing or an activity, which is chosen. Had Voltaire been a bit more conversant with the literature on the subject of free choice, he would scarcely have been able to assert that the fact one never knows beforehand what choice he will make—if this is a fact—entails the impossibility of true choice. One cannot, however, plead a lack of acquaintance with previous thought to explain the contention that man does not know what physical motions he will perform in the very next moment. This is certainly the situation occasionally, especially in the case of a true reflex action; but it is by no means always true. To assert categorically that man is always limited by such ignorance is to make a statement which cannot be reconciled with experience. If Voltaire was sincere in his assertion, if he was never aware of the physical motions he was about to perform, then the only possible explanation would have to be drawn, not from philosophy, but from the literature of abnormal psychology.

The second experience Voltaire mentions as a proof that all man's thoughts and actions are in him merely as in a sort of receptacle of divine causality is that man's dreams are independent of his willing, as are the actions he performs in his sleep, the things he does while still a child, and the purely animal functions of his body. If one subtract these parts of one's life from the whole, so little a part remains, Voltaire states, that it is of little account, and one need not even bother considering whether one is self-determined in the remainder. Even if one grants the absence of self-determination in all these phases of human life, this argument constitutes setting up an equivalence between little and nothing. Nonetheless, Voltaire completes the argument with an imperative: *Concluez donc que le principe universel d'action fait tout en vous.*[6]

------

[6] *Ibid.*

It is not only the theory of physical premotion attributed to St. Thomas by Voltaire which makes the latter unwilling to accept a Thomistic explanation of the divine causal action on the universe. As Voltaire interprets St. Thomas, the scholastic's system admits that God is the first cause of all in the universe, but not that he is the only cause. The second agent acts in virtue of the first; the first induces a second; and the second involves a third; all are acting in virtue of God, and he is the cause of all agents acting. Such an assertion, according to Voltaire, must be answered simply by proclaiming that there is and can be only one true cause. All other "causes" are mere instruments, instruments, it would seem, which are as passive in the hands of the first agent as the matter upon which he worked in the "creation" of the universe.[7]

Nor are the Thomists any more to Voltaire's liking when they write of grace as a special influence of God exercised in favor of a given individual. Everything in nature is under the control of general laws; there is no reason to suppose that the master of the universe should be more concerned about guiding the interior of an individual man than about directing the universe of nature. It could be only by caprice that God would bring about a change in the heart of a man when no changes are made in the general laws imposed upon the motions of the stars. It is derogatory of God to think that he is constantly engaged in giving to man certain sentiments, erasing them, and renewing them. If one appreciates the grandeur of God's laws operating in the celestial spheres he cannot possibly think that the same divine being responsible for such magnificence could be occupied with distributing a *gratia versabilis* to one insignificant nun and a *gratia concomitans* to another. God does not create new winds to rearrange a few straws

---

[7] "De l'âme" (1774), Moland, XXIX, 340. In this passage, Voltaire refers sarcastically to St. Thomas as "the high priest of Minerva." Inasmuch as many followers of St. Thomas, in interpreting his theory of free choice in terms of physical premotion have obscured the Thomistic distinction between secondary and instrumental causality, it is not to be wondered at that Voltaire should equate the two. On the question of the Thomistic doctrine of causality, see James S. Albertson, S.J., "Instrumental Causality in St. Thomas," *The New Scholasticism*, XXVIII (1954), 409–35. See also Voltaire's statement in *Tout en Dieu, commentaire sur Malebranche* (1769), Moland, XXVIII, 96: "It is certain that we cannot give ourselves any sensations. . . . The author of nature has given us all that we have: organs, sensations, ideas. . . . Similarly, it is not we who create movement; it is God who does it. Everything, therefore, is an action of God on creatures."

in the universe.[8] Theologians suppose that God acts according to particular views, but an eternal god without general, unchangeable, and eternal laws is a mere figment of the theological imagination, a god of the kind about which ancient fables were written.[9]

Underlying these assertions that God does not suspend the operation of universal laws is the assumption that God does not foreknow the future, and could not, therefore, have "taken into account" all the particular occurrences in the universe in determining the nature of the particular laws to be imposed on matter.[10] Because God is unchangeable, there could not be any later adjustment in the divine decrees. Moreover, if the divine decrees determining the nature of the laws of the universe proceed from the divine nature and not from any truly free choice, foreknowledge, even if possible, could not alter the laws of nature.

Besides this assumption regarding divine prescience, there was another influence at work helping shape Voltaire's theory of God's relation to the universe: the intense amazement and admiration experienced by the people of Voltaire's time when they were made aware of the mathematically ordered motions of bodies in the universe; compared with this new wonder, human affairs seemed dull and unimportant indeed. It is perhaps only with the development of twentieth-century existentialism that the eighteenth-century fascination with the mechanics of the physical universe has given way to a realization that the individual man is more important than any spectacular stellar display and at least as deserving of divine attention.

Voltaire maintains that the divine plans have existed from all eternity. Therefore, it is absurd to think that prayer could change these plans. If the prayer is in harmony with the designs of God, what is requested would infallibly be obtained without prayer; if what is requested is contrary to the eternal designs, there is no

---

[8] "Grâce" (1764), *D.P.*, Naves, pp. 227–28; "Grâce" (1771), *Q.E.*, Naves, p. 551.

[9] "Grâce," *D.P.*, Moland, XIX, 301. (Beuchot estimates that this article was written between 1765 and 1770. See Moland, XVII, viii–ix.)

[10] Voltaire has advanced what he regards as a proof that God could not foresee the future: what is not cannot be seen; the future is not; therefore, God cannot see it—which involves either an assumption that "seeing" in God is a visual process much like our own, dependent upon the reflection of light from a material surface, or the "proof" reduces to a gratuitous statement that God cannot foresee the future because the future cannot be foreseen.

possibility of its being granted, for it is impossible that God should change his plans. What the prayer really amounts to in the latter case is a request that God should be fickle and inconstant; it amounts only to a mockery of God. Consequently, adds Voltaire, men pray to God only because they imagine him to be like them-selves, capable of changing his mind and being subject to flat-tery.[11]

Moreover, whatever exists is necessary. To assert otherwise is to deny ultimately that there is a reason for the existence of things.[12] That is, whatever God effects, he effects because his nature is such as to determine him to that particular activity. As we have seen previously, God, the unique principle of all beings, could not have been determined to his actions by any being out-side himself, and some determination is necessary if one is not to deny the principle of sufficient reason. Nor could the freedom called the "freedom of indifference" be an explanation, for such freedom, Voltaire finally decided, involves explaining by saying there is no explanation, by positing an effect without a cause, a being without a sufficient reason for its existence.

In explaining the necessity which attends, according to his theory, all the events in the universe, Voltaire has recourse to a doctrine quite similar to the explanation of the principle of cau-sality given by classical physicists. If one knew the position and velocity of each particle of matter in the universe at any one time, then one could, assuming one had knowledge of all the physical laws involved, determine for every subsequent instant the posi-tion and velocity of every particle of matter. As Voltaire puts it:

> Every present event is born of the past and is father to the fu-ture; otherwise, this universe would be an absolutely different universe. . . . The eternal chain can be neither broken nor tangled. The great being who holds it necessarily cannot let is slacken, nor can he change it; for then he would not be the necessary, immut-able being, the being of beings; he would be weak, inconstant, capricious; he would be false to his nature; he would no longer be. Therefore, an inevitable destiny is the law of all nature; and such all antiquity understood to be the case. The fear of depriving man of the use of some unknown, so-called freedom, of despoiling virtue of its reward and crime of its horror has sometimes frightened tender souls; but, once they have been enlightened, they have soon

---

[11] "Prière" (1772), *Q.E.*, Moland, XX, 275–77.
[12] *Tout en Dieu*, Moland, XXVIII, 101.

returned to the great truth, that all is part of a chain and that everything which is, is necessary.[13]

Men are simply machines produced eternally, one after another, by the eternal geometer; machines like the other animals, with the same organs, the same needs, the same pleasures, the same sorrows. They receive everything from the great being and give themselves nothing. Men are a million times more subject to God than is the clay in the hands of the potter.[14] If one denies all this, he is attempting, Voltaire says, to make himself into a god. The choice that one must make, the *parti qu'il faut prendre*, is this: one must either claim to be divine himself or else one must admit that he is wholly and absolutely an instrument of God.[15]

Another reason Voltaire found it impossible to regard individual men as worthy of God's making an exception to universal laws is that the Voltairian concept of man is not specifically different from his concept of brutes, but different only in degree, such that a cultured Frenchman would differ as much from a Hottentot as the Hottentot from a monkey. Therefore, while there is a difference in the value of a man and a monkey, the difference is so little that, if one is not worthy of divine notice, neither is the other. Consequently, the very notion that God should perform miracles for the benefit of certain men was incomprehensible to Voltaire. That God should violate his own immutable laws is nothing but a contradiction in terms. Nor could God suspend a law. The only possible reason for doing so would be that he might thereby improve the universe, but when he originally made the universe God made this immense machine as good and as perfect as he could.

And so Voltaire, in order to show that it could not happen that

---

[13] *Il faut prendre un parti*, Moland, XXVIII, 532-33. "Tout événement présent est né du passé, et est père du futur, sans quoi cet univers serait absolument un autre univers. . . . La chaîne éternelle ne peut être rompue ni mêlée. Le grand Etre qui la tient nécessairement ne peut la laisser flotter incertaine, ni la changer: car alors il ne serait pas l'Etre nécessaire, l'Etre immuable, l'Etre des êtres; il serait faible, inconstant, capricieux; il démentirait sa nature, il ne serait plus. Un destin inévitable est donc la loi de toute la nature, et c'est ce que a été senti par toute l'antiquité. La crainte d'ôter à l'homme je ne sais quelle fausse liberté, de dépouiller la vertu de son mérite, et le crime de son horreur, a quelquefois effrayé des âmes tendres; mais, dès qu'elles ont été éclairées, elles sont bientôt revenues à cette grande vérité que tout est enchaîné, et que tout est nécessaire."

[14] *Ibid.*, p. 530.

[15] *Ibid.*, p. 529.

God would suspend or change his laws to take care of imperfections arising in the universe, blandly asserts that if the all-wise and omnipotent God saw in the beginning that such imperfections would arise, he provided for those eventualities from all eternity. This, of course, is something like having one's cake and eating it too; for Voltaire does not for one moment seriously posit the divine foreknowledge, but makes only an oblique use of the doctrine in order to remove any reason for a mutation in the divine laws.[16] But even then the Voltairian argument does not hold; for, if one grants the divine prescience, then the temporary suspensions or changes of natural laws could have been eternally decreed. We are perhaps face to face again with a conquest of the "mystical" Voltaire over the rationalistic Voltaire, an assertion of "cosmic" order rather than the confession of ignorance one might well expect from an empiricist when there is question of the manner in which God operates on the universe.[17]

While writing of "Destiny," Voltaire is quite explicit about his deterministic theory that whatever occurs in the universe occurs necessarily according to divinely appointed laws. The philosophers have proved nothing by pointing out the alternative to this position. That is, if one wishes to deny that a supreme being has formed the universe according to immutable laws, then one must admit that the world subsists by reason of itself. But in either case, there is no possibility that things should be otherwise than they are; what will be, will be. If one could change the fate of a single fly, then there would be no reason why one could not go on to change the fate of all animals, of all men, of the whole universe. One would, in fact, be more powerful than God, who is unable to suspend or change his eternal laws. The Voltaire who writes this and the man who disagrees with what Voltaire has written are equally pawns of fate.[18] Man does nothing of himself; it is God who enacts everything in man.[19] Many men of deep

---

[16] In the article, "Puissance-Toute puissance" (1771), *Q.E.*, Moland, XX, 298, Voltaire states that it is impossible to prove that God foresees the future; to foresee what does not yet exist is only to conjecture, and conjectures can always be mistaken.

[17] "Miracles" (1764), *D.P.*, Naves, pp. 314–15. In this same article Voltaire expresses his notion of the importance of man: ". . . le genre humain est bien peu de chose: il est beaucoup moindre qu'une petite fourmilière en comparaison de tous les êtres qui remplissent l'immensité." *Ibid.*, p. 315.

[18] "Destin" (1764), *D.P.*, Naves, pp. 164–67.

[19] "De l'âme" (1774), Moland, XXIX, 330.

thought admit that, if one is precise in his speech, he must say that it is the unknown power of the divine artificer and his unknown laws which perform everything in man.[20]

The usual question, of course, occurs to Voltaire: if God alone effects everything, must we not say, then, that he effects evil too? If what are generally called physical evils are in question, Voltaire writes, then God certainly causes them. This, however, he does by his general laws, which are as productive of good as God was able to make them. To ask that God should not cause this type of evil is actually to ask that he should be other than he is, that he should have a different nature capable of determining him to a different set of laws. To deny that there is such evil, to assert with Shaftesbury, Bolingbroke, Pope, and Leibniz that all is for the best, is simply to ignore what is manifest.[21]

Moral evil presents a different problem and requires a somewhat different solution. In a dialogue between two Orientals, Selim and Osmin, Voltaire has Selim state that God permits all the world to be filled with absurdities, errors, and calamities; we ought not, however, say that God *causes* these. To Osmin's query whether permitting and willing are not the same with God, Selim can only reiterate, "God permits crime; he does not commit it." It appears that to commit a crime is to act in a manner contrary to divine justice, to disobey God. As God cannot disobey himself, he cannot commit a crime. Men, however, God has made in such a manner that crimes are frequent among them.[22] How seriously Voltaire intended this dilogue to be taken is a moot question; however, it is extremely difficult to find, within a determinism such as Voltaire undoubtedly posits, any possibility of disobeying. If everything is determined by immutable laws, if it is really God who acts in man, disobedience would seem to be an absurdity. Of course, if one interprets the dialogue as an oblique attempt to show that Christian theologians, who make a distinc-

---

[20] "Passions" (1774), *Q.E.*, Moland, XX, 179–80.

[21] "Puissance-Toute puissance" (1771), *Q.E.*, Moland, XX, 297. Oddly enough, Voltaire is quite Leibnizian in his statement that God made the world as good a world as he was able. It seems that Voltaire either was ignorant of Leibniz' theory or that he deliberately misinterpreted it, as in *Candide*, for Leibniz did not deny the reality of suffering and moral evil. Rather, Leibniz accounted for suffering and evil; not, however, by asserting any intrinsic limitation of the divine power, but by positing an extrinsic limitation in the form of mutually incompatible essences.

[22] "Nécessaire" (1765), *D.P.*, Naves, pp. 327–30.

tion between the positive and the permissive will of God, are ridiculous, there is no difficulty in reconciling the thoughts expressed therein with Voltaire's other statements on the question
of moral evil. Moral evil is such only to man. If Nero assassinates
his preceptor and his mother, this is of no more importance to
the supreme being than is a wolf's eating a sheep. There is no
evil from the viewpoint of God; everything, in his sight, is
merely the operation of the great machine which continually
moves according to his eternal laws. If evil-doers are punished
and made to suffer as they have caused others to suffer, all this is
yet but an inevitable effect of the immutable laws according to
which God necessarily acts. While the ignorant imagine God to be
a king who holds court and metes out justice, or the tender-
hearted look upon him as a father, the wise man attributes no
human feelings to God at all. The philosopher, acknowledging an
eternal power which operates necessarily in all nature, simply
resigns himself to the inevitable.[23] Moral evil, in fact, is nothing
other than natural evil; that is, it is merely some pain occasioned
by one organism to another. Plunder and violence are evil only
because they produce evil in some living body. Therefore, man
cannot do any evil to God, for man cannot occasion pain to God.

In the light of this fact, then, in relation to the supreme being
moral evil can have no existence. Death, crimes, and pain are all
the consequence of the laws of nature, of principles in the blood
and essence of man; there is a necessary concatenation between
the physical structure of men and the actions they perform. Men
no more offend God by their necessary actions than do crocodiles
and tigers. It is not God who is injured by pillage and slaughter;
man can be guilty only against another man. But even this guilt is
necessary, for man has necessary passions, necessary desires, and
necessary laws for the restraint of both.[24] Man, while living his
short day on this anthill which he calls earth, engaged in lively

---

[23] "De l'âme" (1774), Moland, XXIX, 341.

[24] "Bien," *D.P.*, Moland, XVII, 580–81. (Beauchot estimates that this article was written between 1765 and 1770. See Moland, XVII, viii–ix.) It is impossible to assign any meaning to "restraint" in this context, unless it be
taken to refer to the process whereby an idea evoked by passions and desires is overcome by "reason." However, inasmuch as the ideas of "reason"
are also a necessary consequence of the condition of the physical organism,
according to Voltaire, it is difficult to distinguish them clearly from the
ideas generated by passion. In fact, the ideas of "reason" are evoked by
the same sort of passions and desires, but with a long-range view rather
than with an eye to immediate satisfaction.

and ruinous battles over things which amount to no more than a straw, is determined in his actions by eternal, unchangeable laws which include in the subject of their grandiose operation this little terrestrial atom.[25]

As there is no possibility that men should offend God, there is none either that they should give him honor or glory. It is only because men are themselves vain that they imagine God to be pleased with their praise, their good opinion of him.[26]

For Voltaire, in short, the relation that God has to the universe is that of a unique cause determining all the things of nature to their every action, exercising on matter a causality which could not be other than it is, because it proceeds from the divine nature itself. As a consequence of the necessitation of the divine causality, the universal laws by means of which it operates could not be other than they are and can never be changed. What seems to men to be evil, then, is a necessary effect of a God who is unable to affect the universe in any way other than that which has brought about this present universe with its limited goodness.

---

[25] *Ibid.*
[26] "Gloire" (1764), *D. P.*, Naves, pp. 225–26.

Voltaire's "Constructive Deism"

HAVING REACHED an understanding of Voltaire's notions concerning the nature of God and of the universe, and having seen the relationship that Voltaire posits as following from those natures, one can formulate a *précis* of the *philosophe's* constructive deism.

The world of nature has been formed by God from eternally existing matter, matter which is finite in extension, of itself inert, and capable of receiving from the divine being various forms and motions. There are, as a result of the divine causality exercised on matter, diverse kinds of material things, each of which is either itself an elementary particle or is composed of such elementary particles, which are themselves extended beings, perfectly solid and consequently immutable.

There can be no new kinds of material things, for the divine artificer, who fashions them, has acted necessarily, eternally, and unchangeably in his creative rôle. Whatever kind of thing exists now must always have existed; there is no place in the Voltairian cosmology for a theory of evolution. Nor is there any room for a theory of "chaotic" matter, formless matter existing prior to the exercise of divine causality on it. God has always acted; his action must always have its effect; matter is the sole subject upon which his causality is exercised.

While there can be no change in the universe so far as the various kinds of things are concerned, there is a change in the motion that God bestows upon matter. Though there is difficulty in reconciling such changes with Voltaire's theory of God's absolute immutability, the Newtonian pronouncements on the question led the empirical Voltaire to maintain that God periodically restores to the material world the motion it has lost through friction and sets to rights the planets and other celestial bodies which have tended to stray from their appointed orbits.

One final element of Voltaire's cosmology is his staunch conviction that the world of material things gives abundant evidence of final causality. The divine mechanic who has formed the universe is an intelligent being who has ordered the various compositions of elements and their activities to definite ends. While it is not true that everything in nature exhibits final causality in all its functions, only a fool could deny that birds have wings in order that they may fly, that men have eyes in order that they may see.

In the Voltairian world of nature, man occupies no especially exalted place. Man, too, is just a composite of the immutable elements of which everything else is composed. He is not different from other animals except in degree; most men are capable of receiving more ideas from God than are most brute animals. There is no need, in Voltaire's opinion, to posit in man some immaterial substance which receives ideas—a soul—for matter and thought are not clearly contradictory; ideas can very well be received directly into the material composite. Moreover, if one posits a soul in man, one must assume that brute animals also possess a soul, for they too receive ideas from God.

Man does not have any innate store of ideas; rather, he is constantly receiving them from the divine being. These ideas are so dependent upon sensation that man does not receive from God any ideas except those connected with the activities of the senses. Whether the ideas are really different from the motions involved in sensation is not clear. However, inasmuch as Voltaire constantly makes a distinction between the divine activity whereby ideas are given to animals and the divine activity whereby motion is given to matter, it would seem that thinking is something more than mere motion or even sensation, but still an activity of a material being.

Once man has received his ideas, then he can, by means of his imagination, compare and rearrange them, arriving thereby at general ideas, abstract notions, and judgments. The question of whether our ideas correspond to some genuine extramental, material reality is for Voltaire not worthy of serious attention, especially inasmuch as those who have raised this question are the same persons who have not hesitated to affirm that they have certain knowledge of immaterial beings. The *philosophe* cannot accept, either, the assertion of these persons that man is immortal, for man is only a composite of material elements, a composite which is fitted to receive ideas. Once the composition has been dissolved, there is no longer any possibility of receiving ideas, any possibility of consciousness, any possibility of an enduring personality.

In his earlier years, Voltaire made a distinction between "spontaneous freedom" and "freedom of indifference" in man. Spontaneous freedom, he thought, was exercised when the understanding presented the possibility of resisting a passion, and presented it as a greater good than succumbing to the passion. Man could, if his understanding presented the situation to him in this manner, resist his passions; in fact, he would *have* to resist his passions, for his will would be determined by the judgment of his understanding. The understanding would be determined, in turn, partly by the physical disposition of the body and partly by the ideas which would be given to it by God. Or, rather, the physical condition of the body would determine what ideas would be received from God. "Freedom of indifference" was possible to man in matters in which none of the possibilities presented by the understanding could be judged to be better than the others, that is, more conducive to pleasure than the others. This would be the case only in matters of no importance.

Later in life, having meditated on the principle of sufficient reason, and having been influenced by Anthony Collins, Voltaire came to consider "freedom of indifference" as a chimera, an example of an effect without a cause. Consequently, the *philosophe* abandoned his earlier position and agreed with Locke and Collins that freedom is only the power to do what pleases one, not the power to determine *what* shall please one. Moreover, human freedom is unthinkable in a world which is completely passive in relation to the divine Being. It is impossible to have a mathematically regulated world in which one kind of being could, by exercising its freedom, interfere with the workings of the great machine. And, if one realizes that God Himself is completely determined in His causal activity, and effects only what His nature determines Him to effect, it is ridiculous to assign to man, a creature of God, a power which even the Supreme Being lacks. Man is only a puppet of providence.

In such a completely determined world there is no room for moral good or evil in the sense in which these terms have been traditionally understood. God has given to all men two powers, self-love and benevolence, which impel them to the practice of "virtue." Virtue consists in doing to others what one would like to have done to himself; it is what is useful to society. Vice is whatever is harmful to society, the habit of doing what displeases others. Beyond these general definitions, there is little or nothing that is regarded as virtuous or vicious by all men; the particular tenets of morality vary from clime to clime, so that what is considered as a great crime in one country may be regarded as consummate virtue in another.

Man has no special power of conscience. He is born without any moral principles, but with the ability of receiving them all. It is his natural disposition and the society in which he lives that shape his moral convictions. The common man, however, will not usually observe the moral law when it is to his personal, immediate disadvantage. Therefore, he needs the sanctions of physical force exercised by civil authorities and even the added threat of eternal punishment in hell. Whether the threat is based on fact is, for Voltaire, not important, for the masses are not capable of knowing the truth. It is only the philosopher, the man who practices a natural religion, who can be trusted to act in a virtuous manner, because only the philosopher is capable of seeing that such a manner of acting is truly beneficial in the long run. However, both the philosopher and the masses are determined in their judgments, and in their activities. Nothing escapes the completely efficacious divine causality. Men are, again, only puppets moved about by providence. That one man is a philosopher and another an ignoramus is due entirely to the divine determination.

That there exists a divine Being who determines all the events of the universe is evident to Voltaire. The order of the immense world machine can be explained only by positing an immensely powerful and supremely intelligent "creator." Even the wing of a fly is sufficient to prove the existence of God, for the mechanics involved in its construction and the ordering of the wing to the fly's activities could be the effect only of a great geometer, a provident God, an intelligent being.

The fact that matter is of itself inert and requires that its motion be imparted to it also points to the existence of a being who gives such motion, and does so without requiring that he receive any motion himself. The fact points, as Aristotle had long ago noted, to the existence of an immaterial cause of motion. Moreover, matter does not of itself possess life, sensation, or thought. These, too, can be accounted for only by asserting the existence of a being which is supremely powerful and intelligent. And this supremely powerful and intelligent being must have existed from all eternity, for the existence of something now presupposes that something has always existed. If ever there had been nothing, then no being could ever have begun to exist; for, from nothing, nothing comes. While these arguments do not have the certitude of a mathematical demonstration, they are, for Voltaire, sufficient to convince any man who is unprejudiced.

In his attempt to explain the nature of the divine geometer, Voltaire makes use of the principle that an agent cannot give to a patient anything which the agent itself does not possess. Inasmuch as God is the source of intelligence in man, God must be supremely intelligent. Moreover, only an intelligent being could be responsible for the geometry which is exemplified in the workings of the material universe. God is infinite, as well as intelligent; but to say that God is infinite is only to say that man does not assign any limits to the divine perfections, such as goodness and justice.

These qualities, however, are not in God as they are in creatures; the divine goodness and justice are not like human goodness and justice. It is for this reason that one can maintain the infinite goodness and justice of God, while admitting what to man seems to be moral and physical evil. The divine power, while very great, is in some sense limited; that is, God has made the universe as good a universe as was possible to him, but it was not possible to create a universe in which moral and physical evil should have no part. Moreover, inasmuch as God was not able to foresee all the consequences of his creative activity, he was not able to do more than decree certain general laws according to which all events would transpire; it was not possible to God to take into consideration all the individual effects of the general laws; and it is only the individual effects which are, from man's point of view, evil. Whatever God has done, moreover, he has done because his nature impelled him to do it. Just as in man there can be no self-determination that involves an effect without a cause, so in God there must be a cause for all activity. This cause, however, cannot be extrinsic to God, who is the unique and immediate cause of all; this cause can be nothing other than the divine nature itself. God is necessitated in all that He does.

This divine being, eternally existing, very powerful, supremely intelligent, good, and just, is unique. The order apparent in the material world is a sufficient guarantee that there is only one principle operative in the universe, one first cause of all motion, one source of the mathematical laws according to which all is accomplished in the world of matter. While it is not possible that this one God should be pleased or displeased by what man does, the philosophical man, the virtuous man, feels impelled to recognize and adore this unique source of the world's perfections. However, the thoughtful man realizes that, in the last analysis, he knows only what God is not, not what he is.

The relationship that Voltaire saw, then, between God and the universe was one of two eternal, self-existing beings: God and matter. The universe is a reflection of the necessity, eternity, and immutability of the mathematical laws discovered by Newton. God is the eternal geometer; matter is the paper on which he works out his formulae. However, God does not merely trace his formulae on matter; he has constructed from it the immense machine to whose wheels, levers, and pulleys he gives the forces such as gravity and sensation, thereby setting them in motion with a movement which is not necessarily eternal, which may need to be renewed from time to time, but which embodies, nevertheless, the necessary, eternal, and immutable laws of mathematics. What occurs in the universe as a result of these laws makes no difference to the geometer; he has not foreseen the consequences of his laws, and he could not have formed the universe differently even if he had foreseen them. It is even doubtful whether Voltaire maintains that the supreme being knows what occurs as a result of his geometrizing, though such would seem to be necessary if this same geometer is to be charged with periodically renewing lost energy and regularly moving the celestial bodies back into their appointed spheres, from which they have tended to stray.

In short, Voltaire's constructive deism is, from the viewpoint of its relevance for human life, a purely materialistic humanism, except for the recognition that man gives to the existence of a powerful and admirable geometer. From the viewpoint of the empirical scientist, Voltaire's constructive deism is a necessary, mathematically ordered, absolute determinism.

As has been noted throughout this study, however, Voltaire's conclusions have not been arrived at with such profound understanding of the problems involved or with such inescapable logic that everyone who studies Voltaire will be convinced that his conclusions are correct. One outstanding weakness of the

Voltairian system results from the *philosophe's* too slight acquaintance with the great minds of the past and his consequent ignorance of the intricacies involved in the problems he himself takes very often to be extremely simple, problems to which he gives correspondingly simple answers, not knowing that others before him have offered the same answers only to have the implications of their solutions made explicit by their followers and shown to involve inconsistencies or further problems.

Moreover, Voltaire was often the polemic rather than the disinterested searcher for truth. A proposition which he employs in one place to contradict Holbach, he may deny in another in order to overthrow a Cartesian argument. He may in one place deny that a certain thing can be known by the human mind, as, for example, the nature of matter, and then, in another place, appeal to a definition of that very thing in order to substantiate a statement. Though he often remarks upon the difficulty of knowing what transcends the senses, he gives every evidence of thinking he understands the nature of God sufficiently well to explain the manner in which God acts freely. It would not be difficult to draw up an imposing list of such inconsistencies in Voltaire. Quite possibly this is evidence that Voltaire was a dilettante in philosophy rather than a serious student.

There remains, of course, not only the question of whether Voltaire should be categorized as a dilettante rather than a serious scholar; there are other problems concerning his philosophical work still to be answered. First of all, while some of the sources of his thought have been pointed out in this study, a complete analysis of his writings from the viewpoint of the origin of the more important Voltairian doctrines remains to be done. Such an analysis would be particularly valuable to determine the influence which Spinoza, Leibniz, and Malebranche exercised on Voltaire. A similar question would be that of the Cartesian doctrines implicitly retained by Voltaire despite his explicit rejection of Descartes.

In the realm of psychology, there would seem to be adequate material for a Voltairian case history leading to some conclusions concerning the degree to which his temperament and emotional experiences determined the direction of his philosophy.

From the historical standpoint, at least two problems remain to be solved. To what extent was Voltaire's philosophical writing on religion and morality in agreement with his life? And, finally, what was Voltaire's real attitude toward the Jesuits, who had been his teachers throughout the only period of formal education he enjoyed? Was it one which made him contemptuous of the traditional philosophy for which they stood, or was it the ambivalent attitude which appears in his letters? These and many other questions remain to tantalize the student of Voltaire.

However, even when it seems that the problem of Voltaire's general philosophical doctrines has been answered with some degree of thoroughness, it may be well to remember the large number of passages in which the *philosophe* expresses his doubts about the philosophical answers he advances elsewhere with such a show of confidence in his reasoning power. It may be well to remember especially his own warning that no one ought to expect to learn anything from him, for he is himself *un ignorant.*[1]

---

[1] *Le philosophe ignorant* (1766), Moland, XXVI, 93. "Si vous me dites que je ne vous ai rien appris, souvenez-vous que je me suis annoncé comme un ignorant."

Bibliography

Books

Archie, William C. *An Introduction to Voltaire's Questions sur l'Encyclopédie.* Thesis, Princeton University, 1950.

Aristotle. *The Works of Aristotle.* Edited by W. D. Ross. 11 vols. Oxford: Clarendon Press, 1928–31.

Ballantyne, Archibald. *Voltaire's Visit to England 1726–1729.* London: Smith, Elder and Co., 1893.

Barber, W. H. *Leibniz in France from Arnauld to Voltaire.* Oxford: Clarendon Press, 1955.

Barr, Mary-Margaret. *A Century of Voltaire Study, A Bibliography of Writings on Voltaire, 1825–1925.* New York: Publications of the Institute of French Studies, 1929.

——. *Voltaire in America, 1744–1800.* Baltimore: Johns Hopkins Press, 1941.

Bayle, Pierre. *Selections from Bayle's Dictionary.* Edited by E. A. Beller and M. duP. Lee, Jr. Princeton: Princeton University Press, 1952.

Becker, Carl Lotus. *The Heavenly City of the Eighteenth Century Philosophers.* New Haven: Yale University Press, 1932.

Bengesco, George. *Voltaire, bibliographie de ses oeuvres.* 4 vols. Paris: E. Perrin, 1882–1890.

Bloch, Léon. *La Philosophie de Newton.* Paris: F. Alcan, 1908.

Brandes, Georg. *Voltaire.* Translated by Otto Kruger and Pierce Butler. 2 vols. New York: A. and C. Boni, 1930.

Brunet, Pierre. *L'Introduction des théories de Newton en France au XVIIIe siècle.* Paris: A. Blanchard, 1931.

Burtt, Edwin. *The Metaphysical Foundations of Modern Physical Science.* Revised edition. London: Routledge and Kegan Paul, 1949.

Carré, Raoul. *Réflexions sur l'anti-Pascal de Voltaire.* Paris: Alcan, 1935.

Cassirer, Ernst. *The Philosophy of the Enlightenment.* Translated by Fritz Koellen and James Pettegrove. Princeton: Princeton University Press, 1951.

Church, Ralph W. *A Study of the Philosophy of Malebranche.* London: George Allen and Unwin, 1931.

Clarke, Samuel. *The Leibniz-Clarke Correspondence.* Edited by H. G. Alexander. Manchester: Manchester University Press, 1956.

————. *A Demonstration of the Being and Attributes of God.* 8th edition. London: J. J. Knapton, 1732.

Collins, Anthony. *A Philosophical Enquiry Concerning Human Liberty.* 2nd edition, corrected. London: R. Robinson, 1717.

Condorcet, Jean Marie, Marquis de. *Vie de Voltaire.* Paris: Librairie de la Bibliothèque nationale, 1876.

Crist, Clifford M. *The Dictionnaire philosophique portatif and the Early French Deists.* Brooklyn: S. J. Clark's Sons, 1934.

Desnoiresterres, Gustave. *Voltaire et la société française au XVIII͏ᵉ siècle.* 2nd edition. 8 vols. Paris: Didier, 1871–76.

Encyclopédie, ou Dictionnaire raisonné des sciences, des arts et des métiers, par une société de gens de lettres. Edited by Denis Diderot and Jean d'Alembert. 17 vols. Paris: Braisson, 1751–65.

Encyclopédie, Table analytique et raisonnée des matières contenus dans les XXXIII volumes in-folio du Dictionnaire des sciences, des arts et des métiers et dans son supplément. 2 vols. Paris: Panckoucke, 1780.

Fitch, Robert Elliot. *Voltaire's Philosophic Procedure.* Forest Grove, Oregon: The News-Times Publishing Co., 1935.

Frankel, Charles. *The Faith of Reason; the Idea of Progress in the French Enlightenment.* New York: King's Crown Press, 1948.

Griggs, Edward H. *Voltaire and the Heritage of the 18th Century; a Handbook of Six Lectures.* Croton-on-Hudson: Orchard Hill Press, 1933.

Havens, George R. *The Age of Ideas, from Reaction to Revolution in 18th-century France.* New York: Henry Holt, 1955.

Hazard, Paul. *European Thought in the Eighteenth Century.* Translated by J. Lewis May. New Haven: Yale University Press, 1954.

————. *La Pensée Européenne au XVIII͏ᵉ siècle, de Montesquieu à Lessing.* 6th edition. 3 vols. Paris: Boivin, 1946.

d'Holbach, Paul Thiry, Baron. *Système de la Nature.* 2 vols. London, 1781.

Johnson, Donald M. *Essentials of Psychology.* New York: McGraw-Hill, 1948.

Lanson, Gustave (ed.). *Manuel bibliographique de la littérature française moderne.* Nouv. éd. Paris: Hachette, 1925.

Libby, Margaret Sherwood. *The Attitude of Voltaire to Magic and the Sciences.* New York: Columbia University Press, 1935.

Locke, John. *Locke's Philosophical Works.* 2 vols. London: Bell, 1875.

————. *Essay Concerning Human Understanding.* Edited by A. C. Fraser. 2 vols. Oxford: Clarendon Press, 1894.

Lovejoy, Arthur O. *The Great Chain of Being.* Cambridge: Harvard University Press, 1933.

Luecke, Richard H. *God and Contingency in the Philosophies of Locke, Clarke, and Leibniz.* Thesis, University of Chicago, 1955.

Malebranche, Nicolas. *De la recherche de la vérité.* Edited by M. F. Bouillier. 2 vols. Paris: Garnier, 1893.

Meslier, Jean. *Testament de Jean Meslier.* Edited by Rudolf Charles. 3 vols. Amsterdam: R. C. Meijer, 1864.

Le Militaire philosophe, par un ancien officier. Amsterdam: M. M. Rey, 1776.

More, Louis Trenchard. *Isaac Newton, a Biography.* New York: Scribner, 1934.

Morehouse, Andrew R. *Voltaire and Jean Meslier.* New Haven: Yale University Press, 1936.

Mornet, Daniel. *Les origines intellectuelles de la révolution française (1715-1787).* Paris: A. Colin, 1933.

————. *Les sciences de la nature en France au XVIIIᵉ siècle.* Paris: A. Colin, 1911.

Murdoch Ruth T. *Newton's Law of Attraction and the French Enlightenment.* Thesis, Columbia University, 1950.

Naves, Raymond. *Voltaire et l'Encyclopédie.* Paris: Presses modernes, 1938.

————. *Voltaire, l'homme et l'oeuvre.* Paris: Boivin, 1942.

Naville Pierre. *Paul Thiry d'Holbach et la philosophie scientifique au XVIIIᵉ siècle.* Paris: Gallimard, 1943.

Noyes, Alfred. *Voltaire.* New York: Sheed and Ward, 1936.

Palmer, Robert R. *Catholics and Unbelievers in 18th-century France.* Princeton: University Press, 1939.

Rowe, Constance. *Voltaire and the State.* New York: Columbia University Press, 1955.

Schilling, Bernard N. *Conservative England and the Case Against Voltaire.* New York: Columbia University Press, 1950.

Spinoza, Benedict. *Improvement of the Understanding, Ethics, and Correspondence.* Translated by R. H. Elwes. London: M. W. Dunne, 1901.

Stephen, Sir Leslie. *History of English Thought in the Eighteenth Century.* 3rd edition. 2 vols. New York: Putnam, 1902.

St. Thomas Aquinas. *Opera omnia.* Leonine edition. 16 vols. Rome, 1882—.

Torrey, Norman L. *The Spirit of Voltaire.* New York: Columbia University Press, 1938.

————. *Voltaire and the English Deists.* New Haven: Yale University Press, 1930.

Vartanian, Aram. *Diderot and Descartes, a Study of Scientific Natu-*

ralism in the Enlightenment. Princeton: Princeton University Press, 1953.

Voltaire, Francois-Marie Arouet de. *Correspondence.* Edited by Theodore Besterman. 55 vols. to date. Private printing. Les Délices, 1953.

———. *Dialogues et anecdotes philosophiques.* Edited by Raymond Naves. Paris: Garnier, 1940.

———. *Dictionnaire philosophique.* Edited by J. Benda and R. Naves. Paris: Garnier, 1954.

———. *Eléments de la philosophie de Newton.* Paris: Panckoucke, 1772.

———. *The Elements of Sir Isaac Newton's Philosophy.* Translated by John Hanna. London: S. Austen, 1738.

———. *Lettres philosophiques.* Edited by Raymond Naves. Paris: Garnier, 1939.

———. *The Metaphysics of Sir Isaac Newton, a Comparison Between the Opinions of Sir Isaac Newton and Mr. Leibniz.* Translated by David Erskine Baker. London: R. Dodsley, 1747.

———. *Oeuvres complètes.* Edited by Louis Moland. 52 vols. Paris: Garnier, 1877–85.

———. *Traité de métaphysique.* Edited by Helen Temple Patterson, from the Kehl text, with preface, notes, and variants. Manchester: Manchester University Press, 1937.

———. *Voltaire's Notebooks.* Edited by Theodore Besterman. 2 vols. Genève: Institut et Musée Voltaire, 1952.

Wade, Ira O. *The Clandestine Organization and Diffusion of Philosophical Ideas in France from 1700–1750.* Princeton: Princeton University Press, 1938.

———. *Studies on Voltaire.* Princeton: Princeton University Press, 1947.

Walters, Robert L. *Voltaire and the Newtonian Universe, a Study of the Eléments de la philosophie de Newton.* Thesis, Princeton University, 1955.

Waterman, Mina. *Voltaire, Pascal and Human Destiny.* New York: King's Crown Press, 1942.

Willey, Basil. *The Eighteenth Century Background, Studies in the Idea of Nature in the Thought of the Period.* New York: Columbia University Press, 1950.

Wolff, Christian. *Philosophia prima, sive Ontologia.* Frankfurt: Rengeriana, 1736.

Articles

Albertson, James S., S.J. "Instrumental Causality in St. Thomas," *The New Scholasticism,* XXVIII (1954), 409–435.

Alexander, J. W. "Voltaire and Metaphysics," *Philosophy*, XIX (1944), 19–48.

Barr, Mary-Margaret. "Bibliographical Data on Voltaire from 1931 to 1940," *Modern Language Notes*, LVI (1941), 563–82.

Benda, Julian and Naves, Raymond. "En marge d'un dictionnaire," *Revue de Paris*, XLIII² (1936), 18–29.

Carré, Jean R. "Pascal et Voltaire: Raison ou sentiment," *Revue de métaphysique et de morale*, XLII (1935), 357–73.

————. "Voltaire philosophe," *Revue des cours et conférences*, XXXIX (1938), 98–108; 193–211; 289–307; 531–552; 606–625.

Crist, Clifford M. "Voltaire, Barcochébas and the Early French Deists," *French Review*, VI (1933), 483–89.

Crowley, Francis J. "Corrections and Additions to Bengesco's Bibliographie," *Modern Language Notes*, L (1935), 440–41.

————. "Note to the Moland Edition of Voltaire," *Modern Language Notes*, LXV (1950), 425–26.

Dumas, Gustave. "Voltaire's Jesuit Chaplain (Père Adam)," *Thought*, XV (1940), 17–26.

Havens, George R. "Nature Doctrine of Voltaire," *Publications of the Modern Language Association*, XL (1925), 852–62.

————, and N. L. Torrey. "The Private Library of Voltaire at Leningrad," *Publications of the Modern Language Association*, XLIII (1928), 990–1109.

————, and N. L. Torrey. "Voltaire's Books: A Selected List," *Modern Philology*, XVII (1929), 1–22.

Haxo, Henry E. "Pierre Bayle et Voltaire avant les Lettres philosophiques," *Publications of the Modern Language Association*, XLVI (1931), 461–97.

Hazard, Paul. "Voltaire et Leibniz," *Bulletin de l'Académie Royale de Langues et Littérature françaises*, XXIII (1937), 435–49.

————. "Voltaire et Spinoza," *Modern Philology*, XXXVIII (1941), 351–64.

Kinne, Burdette. "Voltaire Never Said It!" *Modern Language Notes*, LVIII (1943) 534–35.

Philips, Edith. "Madame du Châtelet, Voltaire and Plato," *Romanic Review*, XXXIII (1942), 250–63.

Torrey, Norman L. "Voltaire's English Notebook," *Modern Philology*, XXVI (1929), 307–25.

Wade, Ira O. "The Epître à Uranie," *Publications of the Modern Language Association*, XLVII (1932), 1066–1112.

————. "The Search for a New Voltaire," *Transactions of the American Philosophical Society*, New Series, XLVIII (1958), part 4.

Chronological Table of Some Important Events in the Life of Voltaire

Nov. 21, 1694, born in Paris

Nov. 22, 1694, baptized François-Marie Arouet

1704–1711, student at the Jesuit Collège Louis-le-Grand

1717, charged with writing verses critical of the Regent; imprisoned in the Bastille

1718, adopted the name Voltaire

1718, first drama, *Oedipe*, produced successfully in Paris

1719–1720, charged again with writing verses critical of the Regent; exiled from Paris

1722, visited Cambrai, Brussels, and The Hague as a "secret diplomatist" in the employ of the French Government

1726, exiled from France as a consequence of a quarrel with the Chevalier de Rohan-Chabot

1726–1729, in England

1729, permitted to return to Paris

1734–1749, resided at Cirey with the du Châtelets

1743, at the court of Frederick of Prussia as an unofficial diplomat for the French Government

1745, appointed Historiographer of France by Louis XV

1746, elected to the French Academy

1749, left Cirey after the death of Mme. du Châtelet

1750–1753, resided at the court of Frederick the Great

1755–1758, resided at Les Délices, a country estate near Geneva

1758–1778, resided at Ferney, in France, near the Swiss border

1778, elected President of the French Academy

May 30, 1778, died in Paris

Index